D!RTY®

YIDDISH

P9-DDL-750

D!RTY®
YIDDISH

Everyday Slang from
"What's Up?" to "F*%# Off!"

ADRIENNE GUSOFF
illustrated by **LINDSAY MACK**

Ulysses Press

Published by:
Ulysses Press
P.O. Box 3440
Berkeley, CA 94703
www.ulyssespress.com

ISBN: 978-1-61243-056-0
Library of Congress Control Number: 2012937123

Printed in Canada by Webcom

10 9 8 7 6 5 4 3 2 1

Acquisitions editor: Kelly Reed
Managing editor: Claire Chun
Project editor: Alice Riegert
English proofreader: Elyce Berrigan-Dunlop
Production: Abigail Reser
Interior design: what!design @ whatweb.com
Cover design: Double R Design
Front cover photo: Moses © Tony Baggett/bigstockphoto.com,
    woman © Dead_Morozzzka/bigstockphoto.com
Back cover illustration: Lindsay Mack

Distributed by Publishers Group West

This book is for Mikie.

You are the wind beneath my Hadassah arms.

TABLE OF CONTENTS

·····Acknowledgments

I would like to thank Alice Riegert, my editor, who was so helpful, supportive, understanding, and flexible. This book doesn't exactly fit into the format of the others in the series, and Alice always understood the unique voice this book needed to have. Huge thanks and much gratitude to Kelly Reed, who found me via my website, liked what she saw, and offered me the wonderful opportunity to write this book. A *sheynem dank* to a *Lubavitcher rebbe* who shall go unnamed (at his request) to protect his reputation, but who was very helpful, and such a great sport!

A grateful shout-out to various people at the Workman's Circle, Folksbiene Yiddish Theatre, the YIVO Institute, and various Yiddish speakers who helped me here and there with a word or phrase. Thank you, Bella Rabinowitz, for your help and stories. Thanks to my mother-in-law, Edith Berkowitz, and my aunt-in-law, Mildred Litowitz, for their help, suggestions, and encouragement. I am grateful, too, to all the other cataloguers of the *mama loshen*–Uriel Weinreich, Leo Rosten, Fred Kogos, Michael Wex–who share(d) their joy and understanding of Yiddish with the rest of us. Much gratitude to the invaluable websites yiddishdictionaryonline.com and kehillatisrael.net. (For consistency, the former is used for spellings that also account for regional variations in pronunciation.)

Thanks to all my friends, Jane Furst, Wendy Brackman, Judy Witmer, Jan Albert, Bethany Kandell, Dave Wilborn and Jessica Prince, Steve Ference, Gabrielle Euvino, Joey Perillo,

Lino Apone (Shh! He thinks I'm teaching him English!) and many others, who listened, read, laughed, helped in various ways, and offered up their own suggestions.

Thanks to my grandparents and parents, who instilled in me the love and appreciation for Yiddish.

And of course, to my *bashert*, Mikie, the *menschiest mensch* in the whole wide *velt*!

USING THIS BOOK

So, *nu*? You want to learn, maybe, a little Yiddish? Drop a few well-chosen Y-bombs into your everyday conversation? Brush up on the language you heard as a child? Learn a "secret lingo" to speak with your friends? Help bring the *mama loshen* (mother tongue) back from the edge of extinction? Impress your Jewish friends and associates?

Yiddish is a wonderfully rich, descriptive, onomatopoeic language full of colorful words and expressions. But Yiddish is more than just language. It's a window into the Jewish mind-set. It's a way of thinking, of seeing and categorizing the world. Yiddish knocks the high and mighty off their pedestals. It questions authority. It argues. It keenly observes the subtle nuances of human behavior. It's philosophical about life. And, of course, it's sarcastic as hell.

Here's a snippet of history for you: Before World War II, Yiddish was spoken by more than 11 million religious and secular Jews throughout Germany, Poland, and Eastern Europe. Today, it's rare to find an assimilated American Jew under the age of 80 who speaks fluently. (Fluent speakers are pretty much limited to the Hasidic and Orthodox Jewish communities; thus it's pretty unlikely you're going to be using this book to hit on someone who only speaks Yiddish.)

Up until the 1960s, Yiddish was often spoken in assimilated Jewish homes by the older generation as a "secret language" when they didn't want the kids to understand what they were saying. As the *alteh kackers* (old farts) passed away, Yiddish all but disappeared as a first language. Still, many baby boomers managed to pick up quite a lot. Through them, these words have worked their way into English through TV, film, magazines, newspapers, and more, until Yiddish became part of America's pop culture.

Though subsequent generations may lack the broad vocabulary of our ancestors, certain things just feel more correct when expressed in Yiddish: *Mazel tov!* (Congrats!) The *gantzeh megillah...* (long, drawn-out story) or *Oy gevalt!* (Holy shit!).

On the other hand, since Yiddish is no longer a living "street" language, without the benefit of pop media to create and spread new expressions, it's somewhat stuck in the early 20th century. Yiddish, while a very expressive language in so many ways, has relatively little raunchy slang. If you want to express naughty or perverse thoughts or actions, or if you want the equivalent of "smoke a dooby"; you need to get very creative.

Toward that end, I've cobbled together some expressions incorporating existing kosher Yiddish words or slang to fill the void. These are indicated by (*).

So no matter what you are using this book for—whether it's to impress your Jewish coworkers or get in touch with your roots—get dirty with it!

PRONUNCIATION

Yiddish is written with Hebrew letters, and read right to left, but for the purposes of this book, all words have been transliterated, i.e., spelled in English as they sound. "As they sound," however, is a matter of opinion. And you know what they say, "Three Jews, four opinions." That's why you've got your "FinkleSTINEs" and "FinkleSTEENs."

Since Yiddish was spoken widely by Jews, or *Yidden*, all over Europe—from Warsaw to Minsk, from Budapest to Vilna—accents and inflections varied greatly. This leads to significant variation in the English spellings. For example, *ferdraydt* is the same as *fardrayed* and *verdrayt*, etc. Proper spelling in Yiddish characters, however, remains consistent (as spelling does in English.) For example, in English, the word "aunt" is always spelled the same, but pronunciation varies greatly from New York to Texas, from London to Jamaica.

I've transcribed words as I learned them, mainly from my Polish-accented family. Those of, say, Lithuanian or Hungarian backgrounds may have learned these words differently. (*Gib a kik* vs. *gib a kuk*, both of which mean "give a look.") It's an issue of, "I say to-MAY-to, you say to-MAH-to." Who cares, as long as there's a bagel with a *shmear* underneath the slice!

In some words, where a slight change of spelling/pronunciation gives the word an entirely different meaning—e.g., *kapporeh* (penance) vs. *kapoyre* (backward)—this distinction has been noted and emphasized.

Most scholarly works assign one Roman letter or letter combo for each Yiddish letter or diphthong, and use them consistently. Unless you're a walking dictionary, you probably aren't too familiar with this key to pronunciation. For example, the word for "grandmother" is spelled, in Yiddish: באבע—four letters whose English equivalents are: BOBE (although the "o" is somewhere between a short "o" and a short "u"). In many dictionaries, it's transliterated as "bobe" or even "bobbe." English speakers would probably pronounce that as "bowb" or "bob"—so wrong! The word has two syllables, with the last "e" being short. Thus, "bubbeh," or even "bobbeh," is more likely to produce the correct pronunciation. By adding the "h" at the end, it's more obvious that the word has two syllables and that the "e" is short. (The final "e" is always pronounced and always short.)

In some words, I've added an "h" after a vowel or doubled the consonant to indicate a short vowel. Thus, *ibbergerblibbernis* (leftovers) vs. *ibergerblibernis*. *Kihnd* (child) versus *kind*. I've tried to remain as consistent as possible. However, in certain cases, due to surrounding letters or because a word looks like an English word with a different pronunciation, I've used whatever letter combo I think will evoke, for English speakers, the most correct pronunciation, e.g., *alteh* (old) vs. *alter*.

CONSONANTS

Yiddish consonants are usually pronounced as they are in English—with a couple of exceptions:

G: always hard, like "girl" (never soft like "genius").

KH (or **CH**): always pronounced like the "ch" in the Scottish "loch," as if you're cleaning a big wad of phlegm from the back of your throat. It represents the letter כ. I've used "kh" in most words, unless it's commonly spelled in English with a "ch," such as *chutzpah* (audacity) or *challah* (egg bread.) Either way, it's always guttural and never pronounced as a "ch" as in "church." (see TSH below)

KN (or **K'n**): both letters are pronounced, as in *knish* (a savory pastry.) The "k" is never silent. In fact, "k's" are quite assertive in Yiddish. Spelled with two letters, ק נ (see "Stressed Syllables" on page 6).

R: farther back in the throat than in English, evoking a slight gargling sound. To get the right sound, put your tongue against the front of your palate. The "gargle" is more pronounced in some words than others, depending on the juxtaposition to other letters. For example, after a "d," as in *ferdrayed* (mixed up), it's a lighter roll on the tongue. After a "k" or "kh," as in *ferklempt* (distraught), it's farther back in the throat and more guttural.

T: usually pronounced with the tip of the tongue against the back of the front teeth. (Think "d" but say "t.")

TS (or **TZ**): a very common sound at the beginning of Yiddish words, pronounced like the "ts" in "its." This is written with one letter: צ

TSH (or **TCH**): Similar to "watch" and "itch." Few English words start with this sound, but many Yiddish words do. It may take a bit of practice to get it right. In English, you often see this sound transliterated as CH as in *chotchka* (trinket) versus the more correct *tshotshke*. This sound is made from two letters: טש representing "tsh."

J, DJ, or **ZH**: like the "zs" in "ZsaZsa" or the "g" in "lingerie." This sound is made from a combination of three letters representing "dzsh." דזש.

VOWELS

Although there are technically only five vowels in Yiddish, their sounds vary a bit depending on where they are in the word and what letters surround them.

In many Yiddish words, the unemphasized vowel is sort of implied. It's hard to say, really, if it's an "eh" or "ah" or "ih" sound because, in many cases, there's no vowel there. Take, for example, the word for ass: *tookhis*. In the Yiddish spelling, there is no vowel between the KH and S sounds. Spelling it *tookhs*, however, would imply the word has just one syllable. It most definitely has two. That "invisible" vowel can be rendered as almost any short, almost swallowed, vowel sound.

A: like "a" in "father" but shorter.

STRESSED SYLLABLES)))

Regardless of dialect, the stressed syllables of words remain the same. In two-syllable words, the accent is generally on the first syllable ["TOOKhis;" "SHMENdrik"]. In words with three or more syllables, the accent is usually on the second: ["rakhMOnis"](compassion). The exception to this last rule is for compound words where a prefix or suffix has been added. In that case, the stressed syllable of the original word is maintained.

E: short "e," like in "bed" (sometimes written as "eh" at the end of a word to assure that it gets vocalized). Note: The final "e" is always pronounced.

I: short "i" as in "inch."

O: similar to the "au" in "daughter."

U: The letter ו makes the "u" sound in Yiddish, but depending on the word, the emphasized syllable, and the speaker's accent, it varies slightly. Most often, it's like the "oo" in "book" or in some accents, the short "u" in "cup"; in other words it's more like the "u" in "you." In this book I use "u" or "oo" depending on what I think is going to evoke the most correct sound for that particular word. For example, "ass" can be spelled *tookhis* or *tukhis*. I prefer the former in this case because to me, the sound is more like the "oo" in "book." (Note: It is NEVER pronounced "two kiss.") However, in a word like *nu* (so), the "u" is longer (sounds similar to the English "new") and seems to make more sense with the "u." And, in fact, this is how it's most commonly transliterated.

DIPHTHONGS

These are diphthongs in Yiddish because they're formed by combinations of two letters, but they generally correspond to long vowels in English.

A: spelled as "ay," as in "day."

I: spelled "ey" or "ei" as in "eye."

E: spelled "ie" or "ee" as in "feel."

OI: spelled "oi" or "oy" like "boy."

OTHER GRAMMAR BITS

In Yiddish, as in many languages, nouns have a gender: masculine, feminine, or neutral. The basic definite articles ("the") are:

Masculine/singular: *der*

Feminine/singular: *di*

Neutral/singular: *dos*

Any plural: *di*

Yiddish also differentiates between the informal and formal/ plural "you"(*du* versus *ayr*). These, and the other personal pronouns, change depending on their function in the sentence (it's the same as "I" versus "me" in English). Again, I'm not going give you a *gantzeh grammar megillah* (long, drawn-out story) here. I'm mostly using the informal *du* because, let's face it, you're not going to be talkin' trash to your parents, your rabbi, or anyone else who might not spank your *tookhis*. Here are the personal pronouns:

I: *ikh*

You (informal): *du*

He: *er*

She: *zi [zee]*

We: *mir*

You (plural/formal): *ayr*

They: *zay*

Note: There is also the pronoun, *men* or *meh,* short for *menschen*, which means "people," or colloquially, "one." For example, *men zogt* means "one says" or "people say."

Similarly, *yederer* (masculine) means "everyone." *Yederer zogt* means "everyone says."

CONJUGATING VERBS

For most verbs, the infinitive ends in "en" or "n" (e.g., *danken* or *dankn*, to thank). To conjugate regular verbs, drop the "en" (or "n") and add the following endings:

Ikh dank

Du dankst

Er dankt

Zi dankt

Mir danken

Ayr dankt

Zey danken

Note: When *du* comes after the verb, it usually becomes a contraction. Thus, *Vos makhts du?* (What's up?) becomes *Vos makhtstu?*

A WORD ON YINGLISH

American Yiddish speakers almost always speak English too. There is a lot of mash-up between the two languages, even among the most fluent of speakers. This is called Yinglish. It's not grammatically correct Yiddish, but it's the vernacular of (especially assimilated) American Jews.

In Yinglish, plurals, regardless of word origin, tend to be made by adding a final "s." Take the word, *momzer* (bastard). The proper plural is *momzerim* from the Hebrew, but most American speakers simply use *momzers*.

You will often hear Yiddish verbs conjugated in English format. In Yiddish, infinitives end with "n"; "to snack" is *noshn*. In Yinglish, however, the infinitive becomes "*to nosh*." Thus, in Yinglish it's: "I *noshed* a piece of fruit before dinner," or "What are you *noshing* on?"

This book assumes readers want to merely *shmear* a little Yiddish *shmaltz* on their English, so many terms included here are in Yinglish rather than proper Yiddish.

CHAPTER 1

HOWDY YIDDISH
VI GEYTEZ & YIDDISH

Jews are not the kind of people who smile and pretend everything is okay when it's not. There's a very good reason for this! Everyone knows that if you go around bragging about your great day, your booming business, or your fabulous love life, the chances are very likely that God (who of course hears everything) will think, "Hmmm, sounds like that *Moishe* doesn't have enough problems. Maybe he needs a nice kidney stone. Or perhaps a warehouse fire."

If, however, you constantly *kvetch* and *kvitcher* (complain and whine) and make even good luck sound like a problem, you will fool God into leaving you alone in your "misery." Thus, the proper reply to "How's business?" is never "Great!" but "*Oy,* we're so busy...I'm working 16-hour days. I haven't seen my kids in three weeks..." You get the idea.

·····You had me at "hello"
Du hat mir vi "Sholom aleichem"

There are a lot of ways of greeting others in Yiddish, most of them pretty informal. These days especially, Jews who speak Yiddish to other Jews tend to be members of the same communities. They may not be friends, exactly, but usually they know each other by reputation. There may be six degrees of separation in the world at large, but among Jews, there are at most only two or three.

How's it going?
Vi geytz?

What's up?
Vos makhst du?
Literally, "What're you doing?"

What's new?
Vos iz es faren neyes?

What's the word on the street?
Vos hert zikh eppis neyes?
Literally, "Have you heard anything new?"

What do you hear?
Vos hert zikh?

What's happening with you?
Vos mahkt a Yid?
Literally, "What's a Jew doing?" (Obviously you wouldn't use this with a *goy*.)

How ya' doin'?
Vos tut zikh?

What's cookin'?
Vos kokht zikh in teppel?
Literally, "What's cooking in the pot?"

What's with you?
Vos iz mit dir?

So, tell me!
Nu, zog shoyn!
Literally, "So, say it already!" More like, "Spill it!"

KNOCK ON WOOD)))
KAYNA HORA

Should you have some good fortune (and hey, it happens!), and you simply must acknowledge it, you have to be careful that your (obviously temporary) happiness does not elicit a smackdown from The Other Side. You know all it takes is one joyful moment with your guard down, before the Evil Inclination knocks you flat on your tush. You must remain vigilant every moment!

This is why you need to understand the proper deployment of *kayna hora!* Literally, "no Evil Eye," this phrase functions as an invisibility cloak of spiritual protection, at least for the moment, from the wicked gaze of the Evil Eye.

> I hear you're getting married! *Mazel tov!* (Congrats!)
>
> Yes, *kayna hora*, the wedding is in June.
>
> How's the *mishpukheh*? (family)
>
> Everyone's good, *kayna hora*.

It's also used when giving someone's age, lest You-Know-Who decides you or they have lived long enough. So...

> I hear your mother is having a big birthday!
>
> Yes, *kayna hora*, she'll be eighty next week.

In lieu of saying *kayna hora*, another way to ward off the Evil Eye is to spit quickly three times. We're not talking about a big loogie. It's more like lightly spitting a poppy seed off the tip of the tongue, "phtui, phtui, phtui!"

> My daughter found a nice guy and it looks like he's going to propose. (phtui, phtui, phtui)

•••••Oy! Don't ask!
Oy! Frayg nisht!

When you ask a Jew, "How's it going?" be prepared to hear an earful of *tsuris* (troubles). Either that, or "*Frayg nisht!*" Literally, "Don't ask," but it really means, "Please ask again, so I can tell you all my misery without seeming like a total *kvetch* (complainer)."

How **should** I be doing?
Vos zol ikh makhen?
A very Yiddish reply to *Vos makhstu?* It's the perfect preface to a long list of complaints:

> *Vos zol ikh makhen?!* Business is in the toilet. My son joined Jews for Jesus. My wife is having an affair. And this damn ulcer is gnawing away at my *kishkes* (guts).

Not much.
Nit fil.

Could be better/worse.
Ez kayn amol zayn besser/erger.

It's pretty bad.
Nebakh.
See more on this word in the Snappy Yiddish chapter.

Not bad.
Nisht kosheh.

It's all good, thanks!
Ez gut, kayna hora! A dank!

Everything is good, thank God.
Ez gut, Got tsu danken.
Jews often thank God after sharing news, good or bad.

> How are you?

> Miserable, thank God.

·····Feelings, nothing more than feelings...
Gefiln, gornisht mer vi gefiln...

I feel...
Ikh fil...

good.
gut.

better.
besser.

really good.
gantz gut.

so-so.
azoy.
Literally, "like so." It's acted out with a shoulder shrug, a tilt of the head, and perhaps a waffling of the hand to demonstrate.

lousy.
shlekht.

totally wiped out.
oysgematert.

drop-dead exhausted.
shvakh.
Literally, "weak." How fun is that to say! Draw out the guttural "kh" at the end, and it's almost onomatopoeic!

like shit.
vi drek.

·····Greetings
Grusn

Good year!
Gut yohr!
An anytime greeting.

Good day/morning!
A gutn tog!

Good afternoon/evening!
A gut ovynt!

Good night!
A gut nakht!

Good Sabbath!
Gut Shabbos!
Shabbos refers to the time period from Friday evening to Saturday evening, but this greeting is exchanged as early as Thursday.

HOW OLD ARE YOU?)))
VI ALT BIS DU?

Mr. Popowitz is called as a witness in a trial.

"How old are you?" asks District Attorney O'Rourke.

"I am, *kayna hora*, 91."

"Excuse me? What did you say?"

"I said, I am, *kayna hora*, 91 years old."

"Sir, please just answer the question with no embellishments," the D.A. says. "I ask you again, how old are you!?"

"I told you. *Kayna hora*, I'm 91."

This goes on for a while, and now the D.A. is very angry. Judge Spinelli is also losing his patience. "The witness will answer the question simply and plainly or be held in contempt of court!"

Cohen, the defense lawyer rises and approaches the bench. "Your Honor, I think I can resolve this. May I ask?"

"If you can get this trial moving, please, be my guest."

"Mr. Popowitz, let me ask, *kayna hora*, how old are you?"

Popowitz shrugs and replies, "91."

Peace, man!
Sholem aleichem! [al-EH-khem]
Said on a first meeting or after a long absence.

Peace back atcha, man!
Aleichem sholem!
The proper reply to *Sholem aleichem*.

Welcome! (to one person)
Borekh haba!

Welcome! (to more than one person)
Brukhim habaeem!

·····The long good-bye
Di langeh gezehgenung

It is said that gentiles leave without saying good-bye and Jews say good-bye and never leave. From the first, "Okay, we're leaving!" until the last *tookhis* is finally out the door, the actual leaving process can take hours. At a holiday dinner, by the time you've bid everyone good-bye, kissed every *tante* (aunt) and *fetteh* (uncle), and promised to call soon, the hosts are already bringing out the breakfast bagels.

Bye-bye!
Zei gezunt!
Literally, "Be healthy!"

Have a good one!
A gutn!

Go in good health.
Gai gezunteh hayt.

See ya later!
Biz shpeiter!

Have a good day!
Hot a guten tog!

Likewise, I'm sure!
Du oykh!
Literally, "You too!" Formally, *Ayr oykh!*

Live and be well!
Zolst leben un zayn gezunt!

Stay healthy—you can always kill yourself later.
Abi gezunt—dos leben kayn men zikh alayn nemen.

If I'm alive, I'll see you Monday; if not, Tuesday.
Oyb ikh leb'n, ikh oyt zayn du Montik; oyb nayt, Dinstik.

Gotta bounce.
Ikh muz gebn.

Say hi to Heshie for me!
Bei a gris Heshie fun mir!

Call me!
Ruf mir!

·····Be polite!
Zay heflekh!

To be honest, "please" and "thank you" are not the most commonly used words in Yiddish. You might hear them in business, or among people who don't know each other very well (in a shop or synagogue, for example). Among friends and family, however, they're used infrequently. The only exception is *Danks Got* (Thank God), a staple of the Yiddish vocabulary.

> **Please (casual)**
> *Bitteh*

Please (formal)
Zayt azoy gut
Literally, "Be so good." Often followed by an infinitive verb.

Thank you.
A dank.

Thanks a lot!
Aheynem dank!

You're welcome.
Tsu gezunt.

Good luck to you!
Zol zayn mit mazel!
Literally, "It should be with luck!"

·····Well, excuuuuuuse me!
Zayyyyytyt moyyyyyyyyyyykhl!

As mentioned above, Yiddish-speaking Jews are pretty familiar with each other. In other words, they talk to each other as if everyone were an idiot brother or an obnoxious in-law. Everyday exchanges are filled with the snide sarcasm that's often an earmark of family interaction.

Pardon me.
Zayt mir moykhl.

Sorry ; Forgive me.
Zayt moykhl ; Moykhl zayn.
These phrases are interchangeable.

I made a mistake. (So sue me!)
Host du bie mir an avleh!
Note: The "so sue me" is implied by the tone of voice and body language.

Chill out, man!
Zorg dikh nish!
Literally, "Don't worry!"

No problem.
Kayn problehm.

If I don't come today, I'll come tomorrow.
Kum ikh nisht heynt, kum ikh morgen.
The procrastinator's motto.

·····Nice to meet you
Es frayt mikh dikh tsu kenen

What's your name? (informal)
Vi hayts du?

What's your name? (formal)
Vi hayst ayr?

I am Rachel.
Ikh heys Rachel.

May I introduce…?
Tzi ken ikh eikh forshleten…?
Note: The *tzi* has no real meaning in English; it just indicates a
"yes or no" question.

> **Mr.**
> *Hehr*
>
> **Mrs.**
> *Froy*
>
> **Miss**
> *Fraylin*

What's your phone number?
Vos iz deyn telefon numer?

Give me your e-mail address.
Git mir deyn blitzpost adres.

Where ya' from?
Fun vanet kumstu?

I'm from New York.
Ikh bin funem New York.

He's looking to settle down/find a wife.
Er shteyt in shiddukhim.

Where do you live?
Voo voynstu?

I live in Brookyn.
Ikh voynin em Brooklyn.

Send my love to your family.
A grus ayer mishpukheh.

·····What are you talking about?
Vos retstu eppis?

What are you saying?
Vos zogst du?

Do you understand?
Farshtayst?

I don't get it.
Nisht farshtay.

MATCHMAKER, MATCHMAKER...)))
SHADKHEN, SHADKHEN

A *shiddukh* is a matchmaking system in which eligible singles are introduced to each other either by family members or professional matchmakers (*shadkens*) with the goal of marriage.

Er/Zi shteyt in shiddukhim means that he or she is up for a *shiddukh*; in other words, he or she is actively looking to find and settle down with the right girl or guy.

Please repeat that.
Bitteh, zugt dos vider a mol.

I have no clue.
Ikh hob nikht kayn anung.

I don't have the slightest idea.
Fraygt mikh behkhayrem.

I know/I don't know.
Ikh vays/Ikh vays nisht.

I don't care.
A gesheft hob nikht.

Look who's talking!
Kuk nor ver siret!

Cut to the chase.
On langeh hakdomis.
Literally, "Without long introductions."

What's your point?
Vos iz der takhlis?
Literally, "What is the substance?"

What's the bottom line?
Vos iz di untershteh shureh?

What's the catch?
Vos iz di khokhmeh?
Literally, "What is the wisdom?"

T.M.I.!
Ikh vil nisht vesn!
Literally, "I don't want to know."

Go figure!
Geh veys!

"I swear! It's true!"
Emmes!
Literally, "truth."

What a mess!
Oy, a brokh!

Don't even think it!
Nisht du gedakht!
Said when talking about or considering a possible bad outcome.

> **If the company goes out of business and I lose my job...**
>
> ***Nisht du gedakht!***

Who says so?
A voo shtet geshraybn?
Literally, "Where is it written?"

Big deal!
Ayn kleinkeit!
Literally, "a smallness."

It's obvious!
M'zet!

Neither here nor there.
Nisht ahayn, nisht aher.

What difference does it make to me?
Vos makht iz mir oys?

·····The questions
Di fragehs

Who?
Ver?

Whom?
Vemen?

What?
Vos?

Where?
Voo?

When?
Ven?

Why?
For vos?

How many?
Vifl?

What else?
Vos nokh?

Who knows?
Ver vaist?

What/which kind of...
Vuser...

Which?
Velkh

Which way?
Durkh vannet?

What does it mean?
Vos maint es?

CHAPTER 2

FRIENDLY YIDDISH
KHAVERISHEH YIDDISH

Like gays, Jews can easily pick each other out in crowds. Just to be sure the "Jew-dar" is functioning properly, one might slip in a Yiddish word or two and gauge the response. If the other person replies with some Yiddish of their own, chances are good you're both M.O.T. (Members of the Tribe).

•••••Friends
Khaverim

Friend
Fraynt

Girlfriend (or female pal)
Khaverteh

Boyfriend (or male pal)
Khaver

Classmate
Shul koleg

FRIEND (GERMAN) VERSUS FRIEND (HEBREW)>>>
FRAYNT VERSUS KHAVER

Yiddish is a polyglot, a mixture of many languages that includes words taken from various other tongues. *Khaver* and *fraynt* are from Hebrew and German respectively. Both mean "friend" and if you're just talking about your pal, either one works.

Because *khaver* has feminine and masculine forms, it can also mean "boyfriend" or "girlfriend." The difference is matter of context. *Fraynt* always implies a platonic relationship. *Khaver* can also mean "companion," as well as "comrade" in the Soviet sense. This undoubtedly came from the old Jewish Bolshevik days of the early 20th century. A fellow member of an organization might be addressed as, "Khaver Greenbaum" or "Khaverteh Rothberg."

Stranger
Fremder

Homie
Landtslayt
Literally, "compatriot," a critical bond among early immigrants.

To be friends with
Khaveren zikh

Hey…!
Hey…!

> **pal**
> *boobbelah (pronounced "oo" as in "bookie")*
>
> **buddy**
> *boobbie (pronounced "oo" as in "bookie")*
>
> **pretty little mama**
> *mama shayneh*
> This affectionate term is commonly used by older folks toward any younger woman (not by guys hitting on chicks!). Also often used between women friends.

·····Who dat?
Ver iz yener?

Toddler (male)
Petselah
Also slang for "little penis."

Child
Kihnd
Rhymes with "wind."

Rascal
Mazek
Plural: *mazikim*.

Woman/wife
Froy

Trophy wife
Vaybl

Husband
Mann

Mom
Mameh

Dad
Tateh

Son
Zun

Daughter
Tokhter

Sis
Shvester

Bro'
Bruder

Grandma
Bubbeh ; Bobbeh
Or even the anglicized Bubby.

Grampa
Zaydeh ; Zaydie

Grandohild
Eynikl

Your children's in-laws
Makhatunim [makh-a-TOO-nim]
An important relationship, with no equivalent in English. They are (or may ultimately be) your grandchildren's other set of grandparents. *Makhatainista* is the wife; *makhatun* is the husband.

Mother-in-law
Shvigger

Father-in-law
Shver

·····Personalities
Perzenlekhkaytn

Jews are fascinated by personalities. That's probably why there are so many Jewish shrinks, writers, filmmakers, and comedians. It's our tradition to scrutinize people, analyze behavior, determine motivations, and then, of course, mock them and pass judgment.

The beauty of Yiddish is the amazingly descriptive words for a variety of personality types, each with a subtle nuance, like a fine whine. These one- or two-word descriptors carry a world of meaning, painting a vivid picture of a big, fat, cigar-chomping blowhard, a pathetic hapless loser, or a devious, trouble-making gossip.

Many of these terms are so apt, there's no succinct English equivalent. Such words have been embraced by American English speakers, especially in areas with large Jewish populations. Even Scrabble dictionaries recognize Yiddish words such as *maven*, *shmo*, and *gonif* (expert, doofus, and thief).

He/She is a(n)…
Er/Zi iz a…

old fart.
alteh kacker.
Colloquially, A.K.

Mr./Ms. All-Talk, No-Action.
piskmalokheh.
Someone who talks a good game, but never follows through.

shallow person.
pisteh kayleh.
Literally, "an empty barrel."

pushy person.
shtupper ; shtipper.
Shtup literally means "push." A *shtupper* is somebody who insinuates him/herself where he/she doesn't belong. *Shtup* is also slang for "screw," which makes a *shtupper* a guy who gets around.

kiss-ass.
tookhis lekher.
Literally, "ass licker."

mumbler.
bulbenik.
A *bulbe* is a potato. A *bulbenik* talks as if he's got a mouth full of mashed *bulbes*.

wild animal.
vildeh khayah.
For example, drunken college kids on spring break, an out-of-control child, or anyone behaving really badly.

vicious animal.
bayzeh khayah.
A brutal SOB, a murderer, torturer, or member of the SS.

WHY YIDDISH IS A FUNNY LANGUAGE)))
DER GRUND YIDDISH IZ A SHPASIK LOSHN

In Neil Simon's hilarious play *The Sunshine Boys*, Willy, an old comedian, waxes philosophical about which words are funny and why:

"Fifty-seven years in this business, you learn a few things. You know what words are funny and which words are not funny. Alka Seltzer is funny. You say 'Alka Seltzer' you get a laugh. Words with "k" in them are funny."

Yiddish, as you might have noticed, has a lot of k-words. According to professional "humorologists," other sounds that make words funny are "s," as well as plosives such as "p" and "f" sounds. Of course, Yiddish has these sounds in spades, making it arguably the best language to express humor. *Kishkes? Shmendrik? Pupik? Ferkakt? Ferpisht? Shmeckl? Pishkelleh?* Dare you to say these words and NOT laugh!

wet blanket.
shlumpf.
His presence sucks the fun out of any party. There's also a slovenly, bedraggled, messy quality to this kind of person. To *shlumpf* means to shuffle along, to drag one's feet. Also, anyone who dresses as if they've been living in a cave. In Germany, this is the name for little blue Smurfs.

stick-up-his-ass.
yekke.
Israeli/Yiddish slang for an anal-retentive German Jew. Thought to be rigid, overly formal, and uptight, presumably because they wear suit jackets or *yekkes* when even the president of Israel appears on national TV in shorts and an open-neck, short-sleeved shirt.

holier-than-thou type.
kasher chazzer [KHAZ-zer] fisl.
Literally, "kosher pig's foot." Colloquially, "all that."

> He thinks he's a *kasher chazzer fisl* just because he donated big bucks to the *shul*.

·····Strictly women
Nor froys

She's a(n)...
Zi iz a...

psycho bitch/crazy drama queen.
khalayriyeh. [khal-AYR-ree-yeh]

bad wife/shrew.
shlekhteh veyb.
Veyberisheh shtiklakh are female tricks.

hen pecker.
klippeh.

cunt.
klafte.
Refers to a nasty woman, not a body part.

Amazon.
gezuntah moyd.
She's big and strong and can go all night; she'll wring out every last drop of cum from your balls then eat you for breakfast.

voluptuous girl.
zoftigeh moyd.
Zoftig literally means "juicy" and is used to describe a ripe, voluptuous, curvaceous woman who oozes sex, Marilyn Monroe–style. It's also a sarcastic/euphemistic way to describe a slightly plump woman. It does not mean fat, although it's often incorrectly used that way.

old maid.
alteh moyd.

busybody.
yenta.
As the old joke goes, there are three ways to send a message: telephone, telegraph, and tell-a-*yenta*.

nosy parker.
kokh leffl.
Literally, "a wooden cooking spoon." A *kokh leffl* dips her spoon into everybody's business and lets everyone else have a taste.

model housewife.
ballabusta.
She cooks, cleans, crochets, and her sponge cake turns out perfectly, every time.

regular Martha Stewart.
beriyeh.
More than just a *ballabusta*, she's the woman who can do it all. She brings home the bacon (pardon the expression!), fries it up in the pan, and raises chickens so you can have some fresh eggs with it.

gossip.
plotka makher. [PLOT-ka MAKH-er]
She takes malicious pleasure in dispensing scandalous news. She may even tell lies to foment ill-feelings and break up relationships, just for kicks.

witch.
makhshaifeh. [makh-SHAY-fah]
A woman who literally casts spells, or a nasty old "witch."

·····Non-Jews
Goyim

Gentile
Goy

Female
Shiksa

A "*shiksa* goddess" is the blond beauty lusted after by dark, short, swarthy Jewish men (probably because she's the polar opposite of his mother).

Male
Shaygitz

A derogatory term that literally means "scoundrel" or "little devil" (even Jewish ones).

Non-Jewish man
Shkutz

This derogatory term often refers to appearance.

> He has a piggy nose and a blond brush cut. He's very *shkutz*-y looking.

Non-Jewish mentality
Goyisheh kup [GOY-ish-sheh kupp]

Literally, "gentile head." Someone who doesn't think like a Jew. For example, Jews, have learned from experience that there inevitably will come a time when the shit will hit the fan, thus we tend to postulate contingency plans for every possible tragic outcome. Gentiles generally don't think that far ahead. (To think like a Jew is to have a *Yiddishe kup*.)

·····Sad sacks, nobodies, and pipsqueaks
Shnooks, shmoes, un shmendriks

Yiddish speakers have more ways to say "pathetic loser" than Eskimos have to say "snow." You've undoubtedly heard most of them, but perhaps you didn't understand the subtle nuances. Now you have no excuse!

JEWISH VS. GOYISH)))
YIDDISH VS. GOYISH

Comedian Lenny Bruce broke new ground with his famous *shtik* (bit), Jewish versus *Goyish*: "Kool-Aid is *goyish*. All Drake's cakes are *goyish*. Pumpernickel is Jewish and, as you know, white bread is very *goyish*. Macaroons are very Jewish. Fruit salad is Jewish. Lime Jell-O is *goyish*. Lime soda is very *goyish*. Trailer parks are so *goyish* that Jews won't go near them."

It's not a matter of religion but of sensibility. According to Bruce, blacks and Italians are, de facto, Jewish. Jews, however, can be totally *goyish* (think Gwyneth Paltrow and Ralph Lauren).

If you're from New York, you're Jewish. If you're from Boston, you're *goyish*...regardless of your actual religion. Handball and baseball are Jewish. Lacrosse and polo, *goyish*. Cadillacs, Jewish; Chevy pickup trucks (especially with gun racks), totally *goyish*. Sweaters are Jewish; wife-beaters, *goyish*. Chocolate is Jewish. Shortbread is *goyish*. Marijuana and LSD, very Jewish. Crack and crystal meth, absolutely *goyish*.

Goyisheh nachas is the kind of pleasure only non-Jews could enjoy. For example, bagging a seven-point buck deer, opening a tattoo parlor, and winning a lifetime supply of SPAM are non-Jewy pleasures.

He is a total...
Er iz, takkeh, a...

sad sack.
shnook.
A pathetic and meek loser, not so much to be hated as pitied. (American Yiddish.)

doofus.
shmo.
The PG version of *shmuck*. (American Yiddish.)

nincompoop.
shmendrik.
Weak, inept, almost comical loser. Also an affectionate, silly way to address a child who's "acting out."

doormat.
nayfish.
This loser might as well have "VICTIM" tattooed on his forehead.

wimp.
nebbekh. (or *nebbish* in American Yiddish)
Woody Allen, the early years.

Mr. Contrary.
Moishe Kapoyr.
To misquote Newton, "For every action, a *Moishe Kapoyr* has an equal and opposite reaction."

lazy good-for-nothing.
Moishe Kapporeh.
Note the difference between "KapPOReh" and "KapOYR" above.

high-class mooch.
Moishe Mekhuyev.
A guy who lives off the money or favors of others and is thus obligated to them for his existence, such as an "artiste" with a rich patron.

Joe Shmo.
Moishe Pupik ; Moishe Pipik.
Literally, "Moses Belly Button," a silly name, for just about any kind of doofus.

Mr./Ms. Unlucky.
shlimazel.
If something can go wrong, it will…and always to them.

socially awkward clod.
shlemiel.
A misfit, the guy who never gets the joke.

A MAN WITHOUT LUCK IS A DEAD MAN)))
A MENSCH ON GLICK IZ A TOYTER MENSCH

Mazel is Hebrew for luck or good fortune. *Glick* comes from the German word for luck. Both show up in various forms, in Yiddish compound words and sayings. There is no real difference in meaning between the two; however, there can be slight differences in meaning depending upon use.

>Congratulations!
>*Mazel tov!*
>Literally, "Good luck!"

>>He finally popped the question! We're engaged!
>>*Mazel tov!*

>Good luck to you.
>*A glick ahf dir.*

>>I'm starting my new job next week!
>>*A glick ahf dir!*

>Big fucking deal.
>*A glick hot dikh getrofen.*
>Literally, "A bit of luck happened to you."

A *shlimazel* and an *umglick* are both characterized by perpetual bad luck. The *shlimazel* brings bad luck upon him or herself by making bad choices, or because of an uncanny talent for being in the wrong place at the wrong time. The *umglick* repeatedly catches unlucky breaks, often through no fault of his or her own.

•••••Fools and crazies
Nars und mishuggeners

>**Foolishness/nonsense**
>*Narishkeit*

>>**Who are you fooling?**
>>*Vemen narstu?*

>>**He speaks nonsense!**
>>*Er zogt narishkeit!*

Damn, he/she is really…
Gevalt, er/zi iz, takkeh…

crazy.
mishuggeh.

a lunatic/crazy person.
a mishuggener.

a fool.
a nar. (noun and verb)

a scatterbrain/ditz.
a draykup.
Literally, "twisted head." Also, someone who can twist your
head with their *mishegas* (craziness).

an ignoramus.
a shmegeggie.
An idiot so ignorant he doesn't even know he's ignorant. Also
a petty person, a whiner, a loser. (Yinglish)

a space cadet.
a luftmensch.
Literally, "air man." A big dreamer with his head in the clouds,
usually with no actual accomplishments.

·····Movers and shakers
K'nockers un makhers

Big cheese
Gantzeh k'nocker
A guy with an overinflated sense of self-importance who's no
more than a big fish in a little pond.

Big shot
Gantzeh makher
Literally, "total maker."

Squirt
Pisher
A child, lame-o, poser, or a little nobody who thinks he's
somebody.

Blowhard
Trombenik
Literally, "trumpet player," someone who toots his own horn. Also a ne'er-do-well, a human parasite, a phony baloney.

Know-it-all
Kolboynik
The guy who's sure he's right and everybody else is wrong.

A ballsy SOB
Chutzpanik
Someone with *chutzpah*, audacity, nerve. (See page 42 for more on *chutzpah*.)

Poseur
Plosher [PLOE-sher]
Someone who acts as if they're "all that," who brags about their imagined superior taste or experiences or talents. Also, a gossip who just makes shit up.

CRAZINESS)))
MISHEGAS

> Everyone has their own idiosyncrasies.
> *Yeder mensch hot zayn aigeneh mishegas.* [mish-uh-GOS]

Mishegas is everything from a single crazy idea to strange personality tics, delusions of grandeur to sexual kinks. Let's face it, insanity is a wonderful rainbow. This word reflects all its beautiful colors:

OCD: "She can't stand to have the different kinds of food touching on her plate. That's her *mishegas*."

Crazy habit: "She cuts coupons for everything! What *mishegas*! She won't even buy more toilet paper when she runs out unless she has a coupon!"

A wild idea: "He thinks we're going to be able to build colonies on the moon? What *mishegas*!"

A life pursuit that strays from your parents' plan for you: "What do you mean you're dropping out of medical school to join the circus? What kind of *mishegas* is this?"

Emotional baggage: "He's great in bed, but he has so much *mishegas*, it's impossible to have a meaningful relationship with him."

A sexual kink: "He's got some *mishegas*! He likes to be tied up and spanked while wearing nothing but stockings and fuck-me pumps!"

Nouveau riche
Alrightnik
(Yinglish). Someone from modest circumstances who's done all right for themselves financially, someone now *ungeshtupt mit gelt* (stuffed full of money).

Faux-connoisseur
Faynshmeker
In German, this term is a compliment. In Yiddish, it is used sarcastically to imply someone with high-falutin' ways: the alrightnik who's suddenly an expert on polo ponies.

·····Pests
Nudniks

You are such a…
Du bist, takkeh, a…

mega-pest.
tsutsheppenish. [tsu-TCHEP-peh nish]
The boring office nerd you made the mistake of being nice to once, who now corners you every morning at the coffee machine to regale you with intricate details of his bug collection. (Also, an irritating obsession such as those plaguing TV detective Adrian Monk.)

nag.
grizherer.
To *grizher* is literally "to nibble" or "gnaw." A *grizherer* is one who *grizhers*.

toady.
nukhshlepper.
A hanger-on, sidekick, groupie. A dork who inserts himself into your crowd, as if by hanging out with the cool peeps, some cool will rub off on him.

mooch.
shnorrer.
That "friend" who always excuses him or herself to go to the bathroom just as the check arrives, someone who shows up univited at dinnertime or constantly borrows stuff. Also a panhandler or beggar.

constant complainer.
kvetch.
To *kvetch* is to complain or whine. A *kvetch* or *kvetcher* is one who *kvetches*.

What's-His/Her-Name
Frayg-Nisht/Frayg-Nishtseh
Literally, "don't-ask." The slacker or slut with whom your beloved grown child is cohabitating. Why bother to learn his/her name when hopefully it's just a phase and your precious *kinhd* will, please God, dump this loser and marry a nice doctor or lawyer instead?

·····Ignorant boors
Proster mentshn

Ox
Bulvan
He's big and strong but unrefined and not terribly bright, perhaps a prize fighter or a piano mover.

Roughneck
Balagooleh
Literally, "wagon-driver," a foul-mouthed, uncouth man.

Unrefined boor
Prostak
Somebody crass, vulgar, low class.

Fat ass
Balgoof
A fat person with a *grobbe tookhis* (fat ass).

An utterly disgusting person
Ekeldikker parshoyn

·····Dumb fucks
Behaymehs

What a...
Aza...

clumsy oaf.
klutz.

dumb fuck.
behaymeh.
Literally, "domesticated cattle," thus someone as dumb and ignorant as a cow.

simpleton.
Kuni Lemel.
After a literary character by the same name.

country bumpkin.
Chaim Yankel. [KHI-am Yankel]
The guy who just fell off the turnip truck, an ineffectual
nobody, a fool. Also, Joe Shmo.

·····Sleazeballs
Paskoodniks

Sleazeball
Paskoodnik/ika
The most odious, despicable, low, petty, contemptuous
scum bucket you can imagine. And the word is so deliciously
onomatopoeic! Just saying it contorts your face with the proper
amount of revulsion. This word is not so much pronounced as
acted out. (Think Jerry Seinfeld saying, "Newman.")

Trashy lowlife
Oysvorf
Literally, "thrown out," outcast.

Creep
Vantz
Literally, a "bedbug."

·····Assholes
Shmucks

He's a major…
Er iz, takkeh, a…

asshole.
shmuck.
Slang for penis, *shmuck* has a double meaning like the English
"dick."

bastard.
momzer.
As in English, it has both the literal and figurative meanings.

stinker.
shtunk.

AUDACITY)))
CHUTZPAH

This word is often misused to mean simply "balls" or "nerve." Certainly, that's a part of it, and yet it's so much more! Someone who goes sky-diving or works on the bomb squad may have brass cojones, but he doesn't necessarily have *chutzpah*.

What *chutzpah* has that "balls" lacks is the element of audacity, an almost arrogant confidence in oneself, especially when pitted against someone or something bigger and more powerful. What made little David think he could bring down Goliath with just his slingshot? *Chutzpah!*

There is usually a degree of admiration (even grudging admiration) granted to *chutzpahniks* (people with *chutzpah*)...but not always. Sometimes, an act of *chutzpah* is just so over the top, it makes you roll your eyes. An example of this would be the *chutzpahdik* (ballsy) guy who calls up tech support for help with pirated software.

One classic example of *chutzpah*:

Every day, a man passes the same old woman selling apples for 25 cents each. Every morning, he leaves a quarter on her cart, but doesn't take an apple. This scene is repeated daily for several years. One morning, as he plunks down his money, the old woman looks up at him without batting an eye, and says "The price went up. They're 35 cents now."

squealer.
mosser.

hit man.
shlosser.
Literally, a "mechanic."

jerkoff.
putz.
Slang for penis, this guy is limp compared to a *shmuck's* more erect condition. There is usually something pathetic, ineffectual, totally clueless, or passive-aggressive about him versus a *shmuck's* more aggressive style.

hooligan.
nogoodnik. (Yinglish)

thief.
gonif.
A pickpocket, crooked used car dealer, Bernie Madoff.
Genaivisheh shtiklekh [geh-NAY-vish-eh SHTIK-lekh] are "tricky moves" or literally, "thieving bits" (from the same root as *gonif*).

> **His business manager pulled some *genaivisheh shtiklekh*, left him with nothing, and now the IRS is after him.**

mobster.
unterveltmensch.
Literally, an "underworld man."

·····Decent human beings
Menschen

To be called a *mensch* is the ultimate Jewish compliment. It's the person who always takes the high road and does the right thing, especially when it's inconvenient or not to their advantage, setting an example for others.

> **A huge crowd of people and not one decent human being among them.**
> *A groyseh oylem, un nito eyn mensch.*

> **Good soul**
> *Gutteh neshumeh*
> The person who'd give you the shirt off his/her back.

> **A sweet soul**
> *A zeisseh neshumeh*
> Sweet through and through, always with a smile and a kind word.

> **Intelligent person**
> *Kluger*

TERMS OF ENDEARMENT)))
DIVREY LIEBSHAFT

Any of these terms can be used to address someone directly and affectionately.

Gorgeous
Shaynkeit

Boy
Boychik (Yinglish)
Used to address any male younger than you, even if you're 80 and he's 70. A friendly, informal way of addressing a man friend. (Demeaning if used toward a waiter or someone in a less powerful position.)

My beautiful girl
Meyn shayneh maydl

Sweetie
Tatellah/Mamellah
Literally means, "little father" or "little mother." Generally used for children in your own family or affectionately among close friends.

Sweetness
Zeisskeit

Darling
Hartzenyu

Pussycat
Ketzelleh

Beloved
Geliebteh

My love
Meyn leibeh

My soul mate
Meyn bashert [bah-SHERT]
Literally, "my destiny." As a noun, *bashert* means soul mate. As an adjective, it means "fated" or "meant to be."

It didn't work out between us. I guess it wasn't *bashert*.

Expert
Maven

Often used sarcastically, as in the phrase *Ya, er iz a maven vi a bok oyf a klezmer!* ("Yeah, he's an expert like a goat knows about klezmer music!")

Strong man (or woman)
Shtarker

Someone either physically or emotionally strong, or one who acts strong and capable, even if they aren't. Also, a strong man, body guard, bouncer, or mafia "muscle." Opposite: *shvakher*, weakling.

·····Socializing
Zayn sotsyal

Here's some useful Yiddish when you wanna shoot the shit.

Coffee talk
Kaffeeklatsh

Shoot the shit
Shmooze

Ths word has evolved to mean "to socially network." Also used with scorn to describe attempts to ingratiate oneself to the *makhers* (movers and shakers).

> He *shmoozed* his way into a vice-presidency at the bank.

Jest/jokes
Katoves [KAH'-toh-ves]

To laugh
Lakhn

> #### Laugh until you cry.
> *Lakhn biz trern.*

Go for a walk
Gai shpatzirn

TACTILE SHOPPING)))
KOOTSH*

A Yinglish word courtesy of my Aunt Marion, *kootshing* is the full-sensory exploration of available wares; it's an examination of the merchandise, often without the express intention of buying. One might *kootsh* at a yard sale, flea market, dollar store, gourmet food market, or even an upscale shop. While it isn't necessary to actually buy something for a *kootshing* expedition to be successful, *kootshing* is different than mere window shopping. It's feeling the fabric, weighing the heft, sniffing the food, seeing how, where, and when an object was made. You may *kootsch* solely for inspiration or to mentally catalogue what's available where for future reference. It's tuning into the zeitgeist of what's out there.

Stroll aimlessly
Shmie

> We just *shmied* around and talked…

Go shopping
Geyn aynkoyfn

Shopping mall
Aynkoyf tsenter

Tactile shopping
Kootsh [cootch]

•••••Other ways of describing people
Andereh bashraybn fur menschen

He/She is…
Er/Zi…

slow as molasses.
krikht vi a vantz.
Literally, "crawls like a bedbug."

useless.
geglikhn tsu a Chanukah likhtl.
Literally, "gives light like a Chanukah candle," a short-lived and merely symbolic source of illumination.

senile/forgetful/scatterbrained.
iz oyver-buttel ; ayver-botl.

a real motormouth.
reyt vi fyor un vasser.
Literally, "talks like fire and like flood."

strong as a horse.
shtark vi a ferd.

full of him/herself.
ongeblussen. [ON-geh-bluss-en]
Literally, "all puffed up," someone who huffs their own hot air.

just like his father/her mother.
der tatteh oysn oyg/di mamma oysn oyg.

a real prima donna.
a prietzteh, takkeh.

He rehashes everything again and again.
Er molt gemolen mel.
Literally, "He grinds already-ground flour."

He has verbal diarrhea.
Vos iz ahfen kop, iz ahfen tsung.
Literally, "What's in his mind is on his tongue."

Queer
Faygellah
Literally, "little birdy." Some take this as pejorative, but others (such as me) use it with utmost affection.

Faggot
Marty Cohen
This is pure New York Yinglish. A play on *maricón*, pejorative Spanglish slang for homosexual. Less offensive in Yiddish because it's a silly pun.

CHAPTER 3

SNAPPY YIDDISH
GIKH YIDDISH

There are certain Yiddish words, phrases, and even sentence structures that are so frequently used, you've got to master them if only to get the rhythm and flavor of the language. In fact, if you learn only these terms and sprinkle them liberally into your conversation, you will give the distinct impression you speak *di mama loshen* (mother tongue) fluently.

·····Flavorful words
Verters fun taam

NU?

The simplest definition of *nu* is "so" or even "well," but *nu* is so much more than that. With proper inflection and corresponding body language (a sigh, rolled eyes, shrugged shoulders, an open hand, forward lean, and so forth), you can ask any question in the world with this one syllable:

Nu?
What are you waiting for? Say something already!

Nu?
Tell me, what happened!

Nu?
Well, what did you expect?

Nu...
So, to change the subject...

Nu?
Why are you just sitting there like a lump of wasted human flesh? Make a decision already!

Nu?
Move along. Get out of my way!

EPPIS

In its simplest sense, *eppis* means "something." But it sometimes functions as sort of a spice or emphasis, flavoring speech without necessarily adding any particular translatable word. The closest English definition would be "somehow" or "for some inexplicable reason," "some kind," "maybe," or "quite" (even in a sarcastic sense).

Eat a little something, **sweetie.**
*Ess a bissel **eppis**, tatellah!*

For some reason, I can't sleep.
*These days, **eppis**, I can't sleep.*

That was **SOME** movie!
*Now that, **eppis**, was a movie!*

You call **that** a movie?
*That, **eppis**, was a movie?*

Does anyone have **any** idea?
*Does anyone have, **eppis**, an idea?*
In this context, the word connotes "maybe" or "some kind."

COCKAMAMIE

Outlandish. Pure Yinglish. Ridiculous, silly, insanely unbelievable. (Note: This refers to ideas, not people).

> Vacation in Afghanistan?! What a *cockamamie [kock-a-MAY-mee]* idea!

IN MITTEN DRINNEN…
In the middle of everything…

> We're discussing issues in our relationship, and *in mitten drinnen*, he starts talking baseball!

GENUG!
Enough!

> What's all this carrying on? *Genug shoyn!* (Enough already!)

GORNISHT MIT GORNISHT

Nothing with nothing. In Yinglish, this is often conversationally shortened to GMG. *Gornisht* is not merely "nothing" in the mathematical sense. It implies less than nothing. To dismiss something as *gornisht mit gornisht* means it's beneath consideration, not at all what it was cracked up to be. It effectively deflates that which is overblown.

> I was so excited when he asked me out, but once I got to know him…*GMG!*

> Any finds at the flea market?
>> Nah, *gornisht mit gornisht*.

NEBEKH

This word lacks a true counterpart in English. It conveys sympathy or empathy for an unfortunate person or event. It can mean "poor thing," "too bad," "what a shame," "bummer," or "unfortunately." It's also a polite way to feign compassion, especially when you don't give a rat's ass or when you're actually jealous.

> Esther, *nebakh*, is back in the hospital with gall stones.

> *Oy!* Did you read about those tornadoes, *nebakh*, that wiped out half the state?

> Chaim, *nebakh,* can't be there because he has to accept another Nobel Prize.

KROTZN

Literally, "to scratch," but most often used in the Yinglish expression "to *krotz* oneself out," meaning to overcome inertia; motivate oneself to action; get off your fat *tookhis* already.

> I wanted to go to that party last weekend, but I just couldn't *krotz* myself out.

OY

In a single syllable, *Oy* encapsulates all Jewish suffering (and whatever bits of happiness we should be so lucky to find in this world). With *Oy* you can express surprise, fleeting pleasure, surprise at a fleeting pleasure, pain, sorrow, deep and abiding sadness, relief, compassion, sympathy, and so much more. It all depends on how long you extend the syllable, and whether your intonation goes up (+ positive), down (- negative), or remains neutral. It can be the quick, *Oy!* of an unhappy surprise or *Oyyyyyyyyyyyyy!!!!* indicating pleasure beyond words. The longer you hold it, the deeper the meaning. It is often pronounced with a nice exhalation at the end—*Oyyyyyyyysh*—indicating the inability to go on with life or more pleasure than a person deserves to have.

> *Oy!-*
> Hey! That hurts!

Oy!+

> That hurts! But ya know, I kinda dig it.

Oyy!-

> You should have seen the guy who tried to hit on me last night! What a *yutz*! (jerk)

Oyy!+

> Wow! Who knew my knee pit was an erogenous zone?

Oyyyy!-

> That's some nasty rash and it looks like it's spreading.

Oyyyyy!- (with rolled eyes, hand to face, head shaking side to side)

> Can you believe what he just did/said? What a *putz*! (jerkoff)

Oyyyyyyy!-

> *Tsuris* (grief) like this, you shouldn't know from!

Oyyyyyyssssssssssssssssshhhhhhhhhhhhhh!-

> I give up. I just can't deal with it anymore!

Oy! Oyyyy! Oyyyyyy!+

> I'm cummmming!!!

Oyyyyssssshhhhh!+

> I came, and it was goooooood.

RAKHMONIS

Compassion, sympathy, empathy, pity

> **Business sucks. My wife lost her job. My kid broke his arm. I'm begging you, have a little *rakhmonis* and give me an extra week to pay the rent!**

SHLEP

To haul, drag, carry, lug—either oneself or something. As a noun, it means "long haul" or "trip full of effort." There is a whiff of complaint or martyrdom when using this word. A 12-hour flight to Hawaii is not really a *shlep*. It might, however, be a *shlep* to visit your in-laws in Florida, even though the trip takes only two hours.

> *Oy!* That was some *shlep* to Brighton Beach on the subway!

> I *shlepped* six bags of groceries up to the fifth floor all by myself!

> Why *shlep*? We deliver!

SHONDA

Shame, humiliation, embarrassment, a pity

> Forty years old and a *gonif*. Such a *shonda*.

A *shonda fur di goyim* is something shameful, publicly witnessed by gentiles, thus bringing shame upon Jews in general (because, the theory goes, we are all held accountable for the worst deeds of the worst of us).

> **Oy,** what that Bernie Madoff did! It's a *shonda fur di goyim*!

SHOYN

Already, immediately. A word to express skepticism or to cut a conversation short. Often used to emphasize other words or actions.

> **Nu? *Shoyn!***
> *So? Do something already!*
>
> **In shoyn!**
> *Enough of this crap already!*
>
> **Shvayg shtil shoyn!**
> *Shut up, already!*
>
> **Shoyn fergessn [fer-GES'n]**
> Already forgotten. Whatever offense you/they have committed has already been stricken from memory, "it's water under the bridge." It also takes the more literal meaning, "Oh my God…I have holes in my brain! Where are we meeting again? *Shoyn fergessn.*"

TAKKEH

A very useful word meaning "really," "truly," "indeed." While this word may technically be an adverb, it often adds emphasis to nouns or phrases, cranking up the meaning to the nth degree.

> **Now that, *takkeh*, was an orgasm!**
> Not just a little O, but a screaming, thrashing, humping, mind-blowing release that started in my toes, traveled through every nerve in my body, and blew my head off.

THE TAILOR SHOP)))
DI SHNAYDERAY

One day, a Jew goes into a tailor shop owned by a Mr. Sean Fergusson. He is quite surprised to meet an old Jewish man instead of the Irishman he was expecting. Puzzled, he asked him how he got such a name.

"Vell, it's like this...My real name is Heshie Cohen but ven I got off the boat on Ellis Island, I had to vait in a long line. I vas fainting from hunger, tired and so nervous...ven it was my turn, I couldn't even remember my own name! De immigration man asked me who I vas and the only words dat came out of my mouth was *Shoyn fergessn!* So dat's vat he wrote on mayn papers."

From this, *takkeh*, you make a living?
Really? Four years of liberal arts college and you now work as a porn industry fluffer?

She's a *gutteh neshumeh*, but she is, *takkeh*, a *meeskeit*.
She's a good soul, but man-oh-man, is she is dog!

Note: The word is used before the article and sometimes before the verb, but never immediately before a noun. Thus, you would never say, "She is a *takkeh meeskeit*" but always "She is, *takkeh*, a *meeskeit*," or even, "*Takkeh*, what a *meeskeit*!" Or perhaps, occasionally, "What a *meeskeit*, *takkeh*!"

VO DEN?

Literally, "What then?" But the sub context is oh, so much more. When used as a reply to a question, it means, "You were expecting something else?" When they say a Jew always answers a question with a question, 99 percent of the time, this is the question.

Are you going to Florida for the winter? *Vo den?*

> What, you think I'm going to stay up north and freeze my *tookhis* off?

Are you making a nice wedding?

> *Vo den?* What, you think we'd make a tacky affair?

·····Interjections
Oysrufvorts

Interjections are an easy way to pepper your English, giving it that *geshmak Yiddisheh ta'am* (delicious Yiddish flavor).

FEH!

An interjection, indicating disgust, revulsion, or extreme disagreement.

> *Feh!* Look who's running for office.

> *Feh!* Did you smell that?

> *Feh!* You want me to suck what?

GEVALT!

Like *oy*, with which *gevalt* is often paired, this one word can mean so many things. Often, it's a cry of despair, fright, or surprise but it can also mean "like, totally awesome!" or "this rocks!"

> *Oy gevalt!* You scared me! I didn't see you standing there!

> *Oy gevalt!* Did you see the newspaper today? What a tragedy!

> *Gevalt!* This backpack is heavy! I think I just got a *killah* (hernia)!

> *Gevalt!* That sex was incredible!

GUTINUE!

Used pretty much the same way you'd use "Oh my God!" in English, both for good and bad.

> *Gutinue!* **My feet are killing me!**

> *Gutinue!* **That feels soooo good!**

> *Gutinue!* **What a** *ziesseh punim* **(sweet face)!**
> Frequently accompanied by a grandmotherly cheek pinch.

HOO-HA!

"Wow!" A very versatile interjection. Depending on the usage, tone of voice, accompanying facial expression, and hand gestures, it can imply a wide range of emotions.

> **Appreciation:** *Hoo-ha!* **Get a load of the** *tookhis* **on that one!**

Amazement: *Hoo-ha!* Look who got a raise!

Skepticism/disdain: *Hoo-ha.* He wants a raise? Yeah, he'll get a raise!

Admiration: *Hoo-ha!* That was some wedding!

Scorn: *Hoo-ha.* A cash bar? Some wedding.

Hoo-ha. He said he's dating a supermodel.
This *hoo-ha* can be skepticism, jealousy, admiration, or amazement.

USEFUL SAYINGS AND PHRASES
Nutslekh vertlekh

Que sera, sera.
Vos vet zayn.

From your lips to God's ears.
Frum deyn moyl tzu Got's erin.
In other words, God should hear your prayers, and whatever you wish should come true.

I should be so lucky!
Oyf mir gezogt gevorn!
Literally, "It should only happen to me!"

I wish! (May it be so!)
Halevai! [ah-lev-EYE]

> **Your Shmulie got into Harvard?**
> *Halevai*, for our Mendel.

May it never happen here/to us!
Nisht du gedakht!
Said upon hearing about the *tsuris* (troubles) of others. Often followed by "phtui phtui phtui" (three little spits) to ward off the Evil Eye.

Why do you need the trouble?
Vos darfstu di tsuris?

I went to college for this?
Darf min gayn in kolledj?

I need it like a hole in the head!
Ikh darf es vi a lokh in kop!

Stop harping on it! It's over!
Nekhtiker tog!
Literally, "yesterday's day," i.e., "old news," "not important anymore."

Give a guy some room to breathe!
Meh lohst nit leben!
Literally, "They don't let you live!" Said when everyone wants a piece of you and you're being assailed from all sides.

·····Sarcasm
Shpitzik

Yiddish lends itself particularly well to sarcasm. Or perhaps it's just that Jews tend to be sarcastic. For example, many Yiddish expressions convey good wishes or compliments, but when delivered in a snide and mocking tone, they take on the exact opposite meaning.

Zayr natik
Very necessary, but also, "Yeah, like you need that!"

> **You spent $300 on a wine bottle opener? *Zayr natik!***

Gai gezinteh heit (also *zei gezunt*)
"Go in good health" or "be healthy." These common phrases are used when parting, and in that context, mean just what they say. Used sarcastically, however, they mean "Go in good health but drop dead the minute you leave my sight." Also, "Good luck with that nonsense! Do whatever the hell you want to do! You're not going to listen to me anyway."

BULLSHIT STORY)))
DI BUBBEH MEISEH

Literally, "grandmother tale," the kind of outlandish, cautionary story that every grandma who's ever lived—Jewish or not—has told their grandchildren to get them to behave.

Sometimes, these were tales of morality (like Aesop's fables) or stories intended to get children to eat or sleep without a fuss, but usually, they were just flat out ridiculous a mish-mosh of Old World superstition, implausibility, and nonsense.

My grandmother used to tell me, "Don't make such nasty faces! I knew a girl who used to make that *farkrimpte punim* (scowling face) and one day her face got stuck that way!"

The term *bubbeh meiseh* eventually morphed into any tall tale or unbelievable story— from wild rumor to crazy speculation to urban legend. When you accuse someone of telling a *bubbeh meiseh*, you are basically saying, "Bullshit!"

A glick oyf dir!
Good luck to you!
Can also be said about a very small bit of good luck or about a small misfortune: "Yeah, that was some piece of luck you had… not!"

Shver arbiter
Hard worker but also a "fucking slacker."

> He comes in at 10, takes a coffee break immediately, goes out for cigarette breaks every hour, then leaves at 4:30. A real *shver arbiter*, that one!

Gutteh neshumeh
Good soul but also a no-good, stingy creep.

A shaynem dank dir in pupik
Literally, "Thanks to your belly button." A silly way to say thank you. Sarcastically, "thanks for nothing."

A khokhmeh

Literally, a "wise saying" Often used sarcastically when someone says something vapid or dully obvious.

Folg mikh a gang!

"Follow me on my path/my way" or "That's quite a long way." Sarcastically, "Yeah, like that's gonna happen!" or "In your dreams!" or "I'll get right on it…not!"

·····Yinglish inflection and grammar
Beygung un gramatik

In Yiddish, sentence structure and word emphasis are important ways to communicate both sarcasm and put-downs. This unique syntax translates easily into Yinglish, making it easy to convey the essence of Yiddish, without having to actually use any Yiddish.

An example of this is in the use of the word "only" in a question, as in, "He *only* wants to borrow $10,000. Pffft! That's all?"

Then there's derision of the rhyming with "shm," a device common in TV, film, and advertising.

> *Hospital, shmospital!* So long as you're healthy!

> *Love, shmove.* Just make sure you get everything in your name!

Anyone who's ever heard English spoken with a heavy Yiddish accent knows there are certain inflections and ways of putting together sentences that are pure Yinglish. For example, in Yiddish, the word "of" is only implied in certain prepositional phrases without actually being used. *A glazl tay* means "a glass [of] tea." *A shtik drek* means "a piece [of] shit." When native Yiddish speakers speak English, they often import this sentence structure, and thus ask for "a glass tea and a piece cake."

Other tell-tale Yinglish syntax:

Maybe better...

It would be better if you just forgot about that asshole! becomes...

Maybe better you forget that *shmuck!*

You should never know from...

I hope you never have to experience such grief, becomes...

You should never know from such *tsuris!*

You want I should...?

Would you like me to pick up some Chinese food on the way home? becomes...

You want I should pick up some Chinese food on the way home?

You want maybe...?

Would you like to see a movie tonight? becomes...

You want maybe to see a movie tonight?

This is often used sarcastically: Turn up the heat! You want maybe I should catch pneumonia and die!?

By me...

He may be college educated, **but the way I see it**, he's not very smart, becomes...

College, shmollege, **by me**, he's no Einstein.

Stop with...

Stop crying! becomes...

Stop with the crying already...I'm not buying *chazzerai* (junk food)!

Know from…

> **What does he know about** computers?
> becomes…
>
> ***What does he know from*** computers?
>
> And the classic, "He knows from nothing!" means,
> "He doesn't know anything!"

In Yinglish sentences, the subject and subject complement are often reversed to imply sarcasm. Thus, "He isn't a great writer" becomes "A great writer, he isn't." It's the equivalent of saying, "He's a great writer…NOT!!!!"

In direct questions, in Yiddish, the verb is always in the second position, following the word that asks the question. So, *Vos vilstu?* is literally, "What want you?" (vs. the English, "What do you want?"). This leads to the Yinglish practice of turning statements into questions by simply adding a question mark at the end. In English, you'd ask, "Should I buy a new car?" but in Yinglish (keeping the verb in the second position), you might ask, "I should buy a new car?"

Additionally, with a simple change of emphasis, you can easily wring no end of sarcastic meaning from such a question:

> **I** should buy a new car?
> *The implication being, "Why don't YOU buy a new car?"*
>
> I **should** buy a new car?
> *Don't tell me what to do! You're not the boss of me!*
>
> I should **buy** a new car?
> *Or, maybe, better, I should just steal one?*
>
> I should buy a **new** car?
> *What's the matter with a pre-owned one?*
>
> I should buy a new **car**?
> *And add to my carbon footprint? No thanks! I'll just keep riding my bike.*

Thanks to Leo Rosten for the format.

THE NIK SUFFIX)))
ПIK IП DI SOP

As you might have noticed, there are many Yiddish, Yinglish, and even English words that end in the suffix *nik*. If you've been paying attention, you might have realized this ending turns an adjective or verb into a noun, meaning a proponent of that thing or action. It's similar to the Spanish *ista*, as in fashionista. So, one who *nudjes* (pesters) is a *nudnik* (pest). A *no-goodnik* is a rotten scoundrel. And a *beatnik* is one who is beat, man!

Here are a few for the new millennium:

Someone who tweets: *twitnik*

E-book reader: *nooknik*

Couch potato: *spudnik*

Movie buff: *flicknik*

Car mechanic: *dipsticknik*

Tshotshka maven: *knickknacknik*

Someone who's had too much plastic surgery: *niptucknik*

•••••Common expressions
Shprikhvorts

Never show a fool half-finished work.
A nar vayst men nisht ken halbeh arbet.
This was one of my grandfather's favorite aphorisms. It means, a fool can't visualize the final outcome, so don't waste your time showing or telling him what you're doing.

There he stands, a little man in front of a windmill. The blades turn, and he thinks he's the **boss** of them.
*Shtel zikh fur a kortza far a vindmill; di plokhas drayen zikh un ER is der **balabus**.*
In my family, a *kortza* is someone who thinks they're running the show or making the wheels turn, when in fact, everything would function just the same with or without them: Did you

see that cop in the middle of the intersection? He's waving his arms and blowing his whistle, and people are just doing whatever they want! What a *kortza!*

To kill two birds with one stone.
Shisn tsvey hozn mit eyn shos.

Out of sight, out of mind.
Vayt fun di oygn, vayt fun hartzn.
Literally, "far from the eyes, far from the heart."

Lie down with dogs and you get up with fleas.
Az meh shloft mit hint, shtayt men oyf mit flai.

Live to 100 like you're 20.
Biz hundert vi tsvantsik.

If you want to avoid old age, hang yourself when you're young.
Az meh vil nit alt veren, zol men zikh yungerheit oyfhengen.

A man should stay alive if only out of curiosity.
A mensch zol leben shoyn nor fun naygerikeit veggen.
Note the Yiddish cadence.

They're in love—he, with himself and she, with herself.
Zey hobn zikh beydeh lib—er zikh, un zi zikh.

If I were someone else, who would be me?
Az ikh vel zayn vi yener, ver vet zayn vi ikh?

The grass is always greener on the other side.
Dorten iz gut voo mir seinen nito.
Literally, "Over there is good, where we are not."

A righteous person who knows he or she is righteous is far from righteous.
A tsadik vos veyst az er iz a tsadik is keyn tsadik nit.

It helps like blood cupping helps a dead person.
Ez helft nisht a toyten kayn bankes.
In other words, it doesn't help at all. Often shortened to *toyten bankes* meaning, "it's a useless endeavor" or "why bother?"

CHAPTER 4

PARTY YIDDISH
SIMCHA YIDDISH

For most Jews, "partying" does not mean drinking until you fall down. It means eating until you need a colonic just to fit into your muumuu. Where Jews gather, there will be food, but we'll save that for the Hungry chapter. A *simcha [SIM-kha]* is any celebration or happy occasion, from a wedding to a *bar mitzvah* to a birthday party.

•••••Where's the party?
Voo iz di simcha?

Let's have a good time!
Lozmir vayln zikh!

Let's go to the...
Lozmir gayn tsu der...

nightclub.
nakht lawkahl.

gambling casino.
ahzart kaseenau.

concert.
kontzert.

wedding.
chassineh. [KHAS-sin-ah]

party.
simcha.

bar/bat mitzvah.
bar/bat mitzvah.

Where can we go…?
Voo kennen mir gayn…?

> **to dance**
> *tantzn*
>
> **to drink**
> *trinkn*
>
> **to smoke**
> *reykhern*
>
> **to play cards**
> *shpieln kortn*
>
> **to screw**
> *shtuppn*

Hmmmm, this party is pretty…
Hmmm, dos simcha is zayr…

> **interesting.**
> *intehrehsant.*
>
> **funny.**
> *kawmish.*
>
> **crazy.**
> *mishuggeh.*
>
> **silly.**
> *narish.*
>
> **amazing.**
> *ployimdik.*
>
> **pointless.**
> *umzistik.*

NOWHERESVILLE)))
YENEMSVELT

Literally, "Someone else's world." This is a word play on *yeneh velt*, which means, biblically, "the next world to come." *Yenem* means "someone else"; thus it describes somewhere far from your usual stomping grounds, i.e., way the hell out in the boonies.

> That party was in *yenemsvelt*! We had to change trains three times, and then take a bus to get there!

Used interchangeably with *yenemsvelt*, *ekvelt* is what you'd call the suburbs of nowhere. Literally, "the physical end of the world," it's the last stop before you fall off the earth.

> I heard he got into some two-year aggie college in *ekvelt*.

Check it out!
Gib a kik (or kuk)!
Literally, "Give a look!"

> *Gib a kik!* Sammy and Rachel are swapping spit!

Let's go wild!
Let's turn this matzoh into farfel!
This is my husband's original, but it cracks me up every time we say it, so I'm sharing it! (*Farfel* is crumbled *matzoh* bits often used in soup or *kugels*.)

·····You're wearing THAT!?
Trogst du yentz?

Jewish women love to get dressed up. Any wedding or bar/bat mitzvah is, in some part, a fashion show. Being invited to such a party is an excuse to shop for a fabulous new outfit. My grandmother used to feel like a million bucks in her *gom mit secrets* (very broken Yinglish for "gown with sequins.") Of course, nobody pays retail! The competition is not only about whose dress is more fab, but who got the best deal.

All decked out
Vi Chaveleh tsu der get

Literally, "Like Chaveleh on her way to the divorce." Legally, a Jewish man can divorce his wife for any reason. A *get* is the document that the husband gives the wife (never vice versa), stating that he sets her free. Without it, a woman becomes an *agunah* (anchored) and cannot remarry a Jewish man. In this case, Chaveleh is going to the rabbi to get her official paperwork, ecstatic that she will soon be a free woman.

Dressed to the nines
Ferpootzt

Overly made-up
Fertootzt

> Where do you think you're going, young lady, all *fertootzt?* Wipe off that lipstick and sparkly eye shadow! You're only seven years old!

Overdressed
Oysgehpootzt

Overly decorated
Ungehpatschget [ON-geh-potch-ged]
This word can be applied to anything overdone from décor to artwork to fashion to recipes to party themes to...

Bling
Finkl

> Did you see that diamond necklace on her? That's some serious *finkl!*

To be all blinged out
Finklen
Literally, "to sparkle" or "to glitter."

WHAT'S THE PROBLEM HERE?)))
VOS IZ DAU DI PROBLEHM?

I forgot my...
Ikh hob fergessn meyn...

money.
gelt.

cash.
mezuma.

keys.
shlisseln.

purse/wallet.
bitl/bitteleh.

cigarettes.
papiros (or sigaretz).

name.
nohmen.

I'm **lost**.
*Ikh bin **farblondzshet** [far-BLOND-zshet].*
Also mentally lost, i.e., confused.

> I was so stoned, I didn't even know where I was! I started walking home and got completely farblondzshet in my own neighborhood!

A chick showing off her new dress
A maydl mit a klaydl
Literally, "A girl with a dress."

A bargain
A metziah

> It was such a *metziah*! Marked down from $400 to $39.95!

Revolting
Khalushes [khal-OO-shus]

I don't know which was more *khalushes*…the food, the décor, or the bride's family!

The real deal
Der rikhtikeh kheyfets [RIKH-tik-eh KHI-fetz]
Rikhtikeh means correct, proper, legal, authentic, genuine.
Kheyfets is thing, object, article.

> Me? Wear cubic zirconia? I'll have you know this ring is the *rikhtikeh khayfets!*

Old dress
Shmata [SHMAH-tah]
Literally, "rag." The fashion industry is colloquially called the "*shmata* biz" or "rag trade." *Shmata* can mean any rag from the thing you use to wash the car, to that ratty corner of a baby blanket a kid carries around 'til he's ten (often called *motti* in baby talk) to last year's frock you bought at markdown.

Oldy, moldy…
Farshimmelt…
Moldy, rotten, moth-eaten. Can refer to an object or to a person's brain, which is old and "full of holes."

Dirty…
Shmutzik…(like the "oo" in book)

> **underwear**
> *ontervesh*

> **panties**
> *hayzlekh*

> **bra**
> *stahnik*

> **long johns**
> *gatkes [GOT-gess]*

Note: *Shmutz* means dirt; *shmutzik* is the adjective. Thus, "You have some *shmutz* on your face," but, "Your face is all *shmutzik*."

DANCE! DANCE! DANCE!)))
TANZ! TANZ! TANZ!

In religious Jewish circles, men and women don't mingle. They don't sit together in synagogue or on the bus. They don't touch in public. Co-ed dancing, even at weddings, is strictly forbidden. There's no such thing as Prom Night at the Yeshiva.

Of course, not all Jews are religious. While men and women traditionally don't dance together at Orthodox gatherings, there's a whole lotta co-ed shakin' going on at the weddings and bar and bat mitzvahs of assimilated Jews.

Hora

No *simcha* is complete without a hora, in which every guest, young and old, participates. The hora is very a simple folk dance, usually performed to *"Hava Nagillah."* The bridal couple or the bar/bat mitzvah child is usually carried around on a chair, above the crowd, as the guests below hold hands, winding around the dance floor, weaving in and out and around each other. This, and the Viennese dessert table, are the highlights of any large Jewish rite of passage celebration.

Kazatzka

There is always an uncle or male cousin or two who will entertain the guests doing a *kazatzka* (aka "that Russian squat dance"). There comes a time, however, when the torch is passed to the next generation. After 40, you may still be able to squat, but standing up again is a whole other matter!

·····Drinking booze
Trinkn yash

If you're planning a big party with a lot of Jews, figure on spending at least twice as much on appetizers as on booze. Aunt Sadie may nurse that whiskey sour all night, but she'll probably have three passes at the smorgasbord.

Mitzvah Tantz

Men only for this one. The groom, close family members, honored rabbis, etc., dance for the bride holding a *gartel* (special belt) or a cloth napkin. You could get *ferklempt* (all choked up) watching grandpa dancing with all the uncles and cousins!

Mizinke

The *mizinke* is a dance for the parents of the bride/groom, when their last child is married.

Miserlou

Another circle dance, much slower than the hora, and also involving all or most of the guests. The song (and dance) originated in Athens in the '20s and came to the U.S. via Greek immigrants. In the 1940s, Miriam Kressyn wrote Yiddish lyrics to the tune, and it quickly became a favorite at Jewish (as well as Greek and Middle-Eastern) celebrations. Dick Dale, King of the Surf Guitar, did a fast and wild version of it, used in the film *Pulp Fiction* (definitely NOT your grandmother's *miserlou*!).

Mayim, Mayim

It's like the Jewish grapevine, an Israeli folk dance (performed to the song of the same name.) It means "water, water" in Hebrew and was written back in the 1930s to commemorate the finding of water in the desert. It's a staple not only of parties but of Jewish camps, schools, and international folk dance festivals.

Let's have another drink!
Lawmir nawkh a mol oystrinkn!

Can I buy you something to drink?
Tsi mayg ikh dir koyfn eppis trinkn?

Did you come here alone?
Bist aheer gehkumin alayn?

Bartender
Barman [bahr-mahn]

Bring me a...
Brengt mir a...

    drink.
    gehtrank.

    glass of (red/white) wine.
    glaz (royter/veyser) vayn.

    large bottle of light beer.
    flahsh beer hehleh.

    small bottle of dark beer
    flahshl beer tunkeleh. [TOON-kel-leh]

    whiskey.
    bronfn ; viskey.

    whiskey and soda.
    viskey mit sodeh.

    vodka.
    vodkeh.

    schnaps.
    shnaps.

    cognac.
    kawnyak.

    champagne.
    shahmpahnyehr.

    liqueur.
    leekehr.

    cocktail.
    koktayl.

    non-alcoholic drink.
    nit alkahawleesher [al-kah-HAWL-ish-er] gehtrank.

To life!
L'chaim!

To health!
Zie gezunt!

KOSHER WINE)))
KASHER VAYN

There are several special requirements for making kosher wine, few of which have anything to do with the actual ingredients, since grapes (and all fruit), in and of themselves, are kosher.

There is no technical reason why kosher wine cannot be light, delicate and snobbishly good; and in fact, in the past decade or so, several wineries, both in the U.S. and Israel, have begun to offer many varietals for Orthodox wine snobs.

For most Jews, however, "kosher wine" means Manischewitz, a heavy, cloyingly sweet beverage with the heady notes of cough syrup and grape soda. In fact, corn syrup is used to give it its distinctive flavor and "body" (except for batches made expressly for Passover, when corn products are not allowed). Often used at the Passover *Seder*, this is usually the first wine Jewish children ever taste. It's here, they may experience their first state of inebriation, which I call *Manischewitz moyakh* (Manischewitz brain).

•••••Drunk
Shikker

I'm...
Ikh bin...

> **tipsy.**
> *bbatrinkn.*
>
> **loopy.**
> *mooleh.*
>
> **hammered.**
> *fershikkert.*
>
> **sloshed.**
> *begihlihfin.*
>
> **drunk.**
> *shikker.*
> Both a noun and adjective.

dead drunk.
toyt shikker.

loaded.
farshnokhet.

The drunk is drunk on liquor.
Der shikker iz shikker mit likor.

I am so wasted!
Ikh bin takkeh khorev!
Literally, "I am totally destroyed!"

Hit me again!
Nakh a bissel fun dem!
Literally, "A little more of this!"

I've had enough!
Dos is genug!

I wanna barf.
Ikh vil brekhn.

I'm so hungover.
Ikh hob a groyseh katzen-yammer.

•••••Drugs
Narkotiks

While Yiddish has words for smoking and various kinds of drinks, there are no words for harder drugs. This is not to say that those who speak Yiddish would never do such things (exhibit A: Lenny Bruce). It's just that such things as cocaine, crack, Ecstasy, and even marijuana didn't exist back in the day in Minsk. These are mostly New World debaucheries, so if you're toking or snorting, you'll be doing it in the local vernacular.

Hash
Hashish

Grass
*Graz**

Weed
*Vildgraz**
Literally, "wild grass" or weed.

Wacky tobaccy
*Mishuggedikh tabak**

Garbage weed
*Chazzerai** [khaz-zer-EYE]
Literally, "pig slop." Commonly used to mean any inferior product, foodstuff, junk food, or even nonsense.

Skunk weed
*Shtunk**

Joint
*Ferdrayed papiros**
Literally, "twisted cigarette."
Ferdrayed means "twisted" both literally and in the "crazy, mixed up" sense of the word, so it's perfect slang for a joint.

Doobie
*Shtik graz**
Literally, a "stick of grass."

Mushrooms
Shvemlekh

Magic mushrooms
*Kishefdik shvemlekh** [KISH-ef-dik SHVEM-lekh]

Coke
*Shney**
Literally, "snow."

LSD
*LamSamDal**
Short for Lamed Samekh Daled, the Hebrew letters L-S-D.

Opium
Opiyom

Cigarette
Papiros

Pipe
Pipke

Lighter
Ontsinder

Can you give me a light, please?
*Git mir a **fyer**, zayt azoy gut?*

Take a hit.
Khop a klop. *

•••••Stoned
Fleishig

Fleishig is a colloquialism that means stoned or high on any substance (drugs or drink). It's an obtuse reference to the "long-term effects" of eating meat (*fleish*). According to the laws of *Kashruth* (Kosher), one must wait a minimum of six hours after eating meat before consuming any milk products. Thus, when you make yourself "meaty," you'll be "under the influence" for a long time.

To get stoned
Makhn zikh fleishig

High
Mevihsim

> Let's go get **high.**
> *Lomer gayn **mevihsim** vern.*

Do you want to smoke a little something?
*Viln tsu **reykern** a bissel eppis?*

Baked
Mastool
From Hebrew slang.

Freakin' out
Takkeh meshuggeh
Literally, "really crazy."

Munchies
*Noshkees**

> That weed was good, but now I have some wicked **noshkees**.

You're harshing my mellow, man.
Du makhts mir dershlogn.
Literally, "You're beating me down."

Chill out!
Opruen zikh!
Literally, "Relax yourself!"

Stash
*Knipl**
Refers to a "nest egg," which housewives saved from the family budget.

Dime bag
*Peckel**
Literally, "little package," also a backpack, hunchback's hump, or even a "bun in the oven."

·····Holidays
Yontovim

Most Jewish holidays can be boiled down to this: "They tried to kill us, we won, let's eat." Except for the fasting holidays. There are quite a few of those, but then, of course, there's the break-fast, so yeah, I guess it *is* all about the eating.

Jewish holidays begin at sundown the night before, *erev yontif* (holiday eve). They follow the Hebrew calendar, which doesn't line up with the Gregorian calendar, which is why they move around so much. One year Chanukah comes in late November, the next year, it's after Christmas. Of course, it's much more Jewish when it comes after Christmas because then we Jews benefit from all those after-Christmas sales!

Happy [Jewish] holiday!
Gut Yontif!

Happy [non-religious or not-Jewish] holiday!
Hag samayakh! [sum-MAY-akh]

Happy New Year!
A gliklekhn nay yohr!
Literally, "A lucky new year!"

Good, sweet year!
Shana tova!
A typical greeting around the Jewish new year.

Sweet Passover!
Zeissen Pesach!

Good Sabbath!
Gut Shabbos!

Happy Birthday!
Mazel tov tsum geboyrentog!

Rosh Hashonah
New Year. Literally, "Head of the year," one of the two most important holidays, along with *Yom Kippur*. Together, these are the "High Holidays," which has nothing to do with smokin' a doob in the parking lot of the *shul* with your pals from Hebrew school. Two days of repentance, *shofar* blowing, and lots of eating.

Yom Kippur
Day of Atonement. This is when God decides who will live and die in the coming year. It's your last chance to convince Him you're a

decent enough human being to live until next *Yom Kippur*. Lots of praying, chest beating, and total abstinence from nookie, bathing, and all food and water. The mother of all Jewish fast days.

Shemini Atzeret
This is one of the most obscure holidays and I have no idea what it's about. I suggest telling your boss you're an observant Jew, and then insist on getting a paid day off. And don't worry if a co-worker sees you at the mall or at a game. Just tell 'em it's part of the observance. Who's gonna argue? Even my rabbi doesn't know what this holiday is about!

Sukkot
During *Sukkot* (or *Sukkos*), Jews build outdoor huts or booths (*sukkot*)—in backyards, on city rooftops, in alleyways—to commemorate the 40 years the ancient Israelites spent wandering the desert, living in temporary shelters, (wandering for four decades, no doubt, because, God forbid, Moses should ask for directions!). During this week-long festival, feasts and parties are held in the *sukkah* (singular of *sukkot*).

THE FOUR QUESTIONS)))
DI FIYR KASHEHS

At the *Seder*, the youngest guest asks *Di Fiyr Kashehs*, "Why is this night different from all other nights? It begins, (in Aramaic) "*Mah nishtanah...*" This expression is used year round, sarcastically, to mean, "What else is new?!"

> The slutty girl says, "I got wasted last night and woke up in some strange dude's bed..."
>
> Her friend, who's heard this story many times before, rolls her eyes and says, "*Mah nishtanah?*"

Chanukah

The Festival of Lights commemorates the historic victory of Judah Macabbee and his band of merry men over the Syrian-Greeks and the subsequent rededication of the temple in Jerusalem. They discovered only enough oil to relight the eternal flame for one day but, the story goes, by a miracle, it lasted eight nights. Jews celebrate by lighting candles on a *menorah* (eight-branched candelabra), increasing by one candle per night, and eating oily delicacies such as *latkes* (potato pancakes). Chanukah isn't the most significant holiday, but because of its proximity to Christmas, it's become more prominent in the U.S., especially for children. With all their *goyishe* (gentile) friends getting the latest toys, we wouldn't want little David and Rebecca to feel left out!

Pesach

Passover. The holiday begins with two nights of *Seder*, Hebrew for "order." This traditional ritual dinner recalls the liberation of the ancient Israelites from slavery and their exodus from Egypt. A collection of texts, songs, blessings, and history is read by guests from a *haggadah*, Hebrew for "the telling." Some families take hours to work through the story, exploring the deep spiritual and psychological aspects of the holiday. Other families have more fun with it, performing skits and using silly props to recall the Ten Plagues of Egypt. These days, there are a variety of *Haggadahs* to choose from—some geared toward children, others with a feminist, political, or New Age bent (for more on *Pesach* see the Hungry Yiddish chapter).

PARTY TALK)))
SIMCHA SHMOOZN

At every wedding, bar or bat mitzvah, or *bris* (circumcision), you'll hear at least a couple of these phrases.

Congratulations!
Mazel tov!
Literally, "Good luck!"

Shep nakhes [shep NAKH-ess]
To derive pleasure from the achievements of your kids or grandkids. When you *shep nakhes*, you *kvell* (see below).

> I wish that kid would figure out what he wants to do with his life. I should only *shep* a little *nakhes* from him.

Kvelln
To swell with pride from the achievements of your loved ones, usually children or grandchildren. (You don't *kvell* from your own achievements.)

> My David gave such a beautiful speech at his bar mitzvah! I was *kvelling*!

Im yirtzeh Hashem bi dir [Eem EERTS-say-Ha-shem by deer]
Literally, "If God wills it, by you," often shortened to *Mirtsa Hashem*. Customarily said to the parents of single adults or directly to singles. In other words, "May you be making a wedding yourself, soon," or "I wish upon you this same happiness." Often shortened to *Mirtsa Hashem*.

Alav HaSholem [Ah-LAV Ha-SHAW-lehm]/Aleya HaSholem [Ah-LAY-ah Ha-SHAW-lehm]
May he/she rest in peace.
Literally, "The peace upon him/her."

> Benji looks just like his grandpa Sam, *alav hasholem*.

Purim

The Story of Queen Esther, who, in ancient Persia, saved the Jews from destruction by the genocidal Haman. Despite the historical heaviness, *Purim* is actually a blast. Jews, young and old, attend school, synagogue, and parties dressed in costumes of all kinds—from biblical characters to modern superheroes. As the whole long, drawn-out story (*megillah*) is told, everyone shakes their noisemakers (*groggers*) whenever Haman's name is mentioned. The traditional *Purim* treat is *hamantashen*—a triangular pastry with an open center, filled with jam—which represents Haman's hat, pocket, or ears. Tradition also dictates getting so drunk you can't tell the difference between evil Haman and the hero of our story, Esther's uncle Mordechai.

Shavuot

Literally, "weeks." Commemorates the giving of the Torah to the Jewish people, seven weeks after the exodus from Egypt. Traditionally, dairy foods are eaten on *Shavuot*, representing the spiritual nourishment of the Torah, putting many lactose-intolerant Yidden at severe risk of gastro-intestinal distress. *Mah nishtanah?*

Tisha B'Av

Literally, "Ninth of Av." An intense 25 hours of fasting, refraining from bathing, *shtupping*, and other ways of afflicting one's soul to commemorate the destruction of the ancient temple in Jerusalem and all the many other horrible atrocities that have befallen the Jews throughout their history. Please…don't get me started!

CHAPTER 5

BODY YIDDISH
KERPEHR YIDDISH

·····Beauty
Shaynkeit

I won't say Jews are never vain. After all, nose jobs were once a virtual right of passage for girls of a certain generation. Yiddish culture, however, is much less obsessed. Most compliments have to do with one's character, intelligence, or inner beauty. Even insults about one's physical attributes generally tend to be more about the ugliness of one's behavior than their appearance.

He/She is...
Er/Zi iz...

handsome/pretty.
shayn/eh.

fine.
azoy feyn/eh.

gorgeous.
hiderdik/eh.

a real stunner.
a zelteneh shaynheit.

THE FACE)))
DOS PUNIM

Beautiful face
Shayneh punim

Sweet face
Zeisseh punim

Shining face
Likhtikeh punim
Said of a righteous or charming person who can light up a room
simply by their presence.

Friendly/familiar face
Haymisheh punim

Pizza face
Ferprishteh punim

Scowling, twisted face
Ferkrimpteh punim

a hot babe.
a krasavitseh.
Russian/Yiddish.

a beautiful Jew.
a shayneh Yid.
A kind and decent human being.

He/She's got it all!
Er/Zi iz mushlemmehs bekhol hamaylehs!
Literally, "He/she is complete in every virtue."

Charm trumps beauty. (Saying)
Khayn gayt iber shayn.

**A beautiful person is nice to look at, but it's better to
live with a smart one. (Proverb)**
*Oyf a shaynem iz gut tsu kukn, mit z' a klugn iz gut tsu
lebn.*

He/She has (a) nice...
Er/Zi hot (a) shayneh...

smile.
shmaykhl.
Not to be confused with *shmeckel* (little penis). Note the guttural "kh" in the middle of this word.

skin.
hoyt.

hair.
hooer.

She has **sexy legs**.
*Zi hot **yetzer-horeh fislakh**.*
Yetzer-horeh literally means "evil inclination," i.e., passion, lust. A hickey is a *yetzer-horeh bleterl*, an "evil impulse blotch."

·····Ugliness
Meeskeit

That ho' is...
Yener zoyneh iz...

That fucker is straight...
Yener yentzer iz takkeh...

ugly inside and out.
heslekh.
This is an ugliness of the soul, a way to describe a hateful person.

disgusting.
vredneh.

loathsome.
bridkeh.

nasty.
paskudneh.
Beauty is skin deep, but *paskudneh*-ugly goes clear down to the bones.

An ugly chick hates the mirror. (Proverb)
*A **meeseh moyd** hot faynt dem shpeigl.*

No one sees his own hunchback. (Proverb)
*Kayner zayt nisht zayn eigener **hoyker**.*
Everyone is blind to their own faults.

He/She is…
Er/Zi iz

> **a real dog.**
> *a rikhtikeh meeskeit.*
> Literally, "a real ugliness."

> **a slob.**
> *a zhlub.*
> Usually lacking in self-respect but never lacking for food stains on the clothing or dandruff on the shoulders.

> **a pig.**
> *chazzer. [KHAZ-zer]*
> Literally, "a pig," or anyone who behaves like one, for example in their dining, spending, or personal grooming habits.

> **a gross dude.**
> *a grobbeh yung.*
> Literally, "a crude young guy."

>> **That new intern is always burping, farting, and picking his nose! What a *grobbeh yung*!**

A piece of meat with two eyes!
A shtik flaysh mit tsvei oygn!
A sorry excuse for a human being.

·····Other body parts
Ander opteyln fun der guf

Brains
Moyakh

Mouth
Moyl

Big/clumsy/grabby hands
Lapehs
Used the way we use "paws" in English.

> Keep your *lapehs* to yourself!

Bulging biceps
Challah ahrems*
They look like big, braided loaves of challah.

Flabby arms
Hadassah ahrems
In Yinglish, known as "*Hadassah arms.*" In other words, flibbety, jibbety upper arms that flap in the breeze, like sheets on a clothesline. The biceps of your Great Aunt Frieda.

Thighs
Poulkies

> **I raised my staff like Moses, and her thighs parted like the Red Sea.**
> *Ikh hob oyfgehoygen meyn shtikn vi Moishe, un zi ungeshpaltn eer **poulkes** vi der Roiteh Yahm.*

Belly button
Pupik ; Pipik

Mole
Borifka

My grandmother always used this to refer to a black skin mole. We all assumed that was the proper word for it. It was only a few years ago that I discovered it literally means "blueberry." I'm not sure if she made this up or if it's common slang, but it's such an apt word (and fun to say), I thought I'd share it.

Is that a mole on your face?
*Iz yener a **borifka** ofn deyn punim?*

·····Rear end
Hintn

Fanny
Tush

Heinie
Tushie

Buttocks
Zitzer
Literally, "seat."

Rump
Zitzfleish
Literally, "sit meat," the tush glue or perseverance to sit for a long time and get the job done.

Aaron needs way more *zitzfleish* to finish that doctoral thesis.

Ass
Tookhis

You can't dance at two weddings with one ass. (Proverb)
*Mit eyn **tookhis** ken men nit tantzn oyf tsvey chassenehs. [KHAS-sen-ahs]*
In other words, you can't be in two places at once.

Meaty ass
Fleishik tookhis

Big ass
Groys tookhis

An ass and a half
A tookhis un a halb

·····Breasts
Bristin

Bosom
Boozem

Tits
Tsitskes

Boobs
Pazookheh

Hooters
Dadaim
Biblical Hebrew for "mandrakes."

Sweater sisters
Sveter shvesters*

Deflated boobs
Latkes*
Basically, pancakes.

Melons
Melonen*

Flesh pillows
Flaysh kishns*

Small but firm boobs
Knaidlakh*
Matzoh balls.

Flat as a board
Matzoh bristen*

A nice pair
Di Rosenbergs*
Literally, "pink mountains," thus large, rosy tits.

> **Here comes Rachel and *Di Rosenbergs*.**

Nipples
Oplen

·····Sick
Krenk

Jews are a bit obsessed with health. Maybe that's why it's so important that one's children become doctors (or at least marry one!). Many greetings and farewells bid good health. To a *Yid*, it doesn't matter how rich or successful you are, if you don't have your health, you've got nothing. Serious and fatal diseases are merely whispered about or referred to by euphemism, lest just by speaking their names, they may manifest themselves in the body.

Illness
Krenkheit
Yes, Walter Cronkite's name means "sickness."

A long, drawn-out illness
Farhshlepteh krenk
Also means a long, drawn-out proceeding, like the OJ Simpson trial.

A sickly person
Kolyekeh
Literally, "one with colic." A weak or crippled person. Also someone who sucks at their job.

Doc, what's wrong with me?
Doktor, vos iz meyn krenkheit?

GUTS)))
KISHKES

Kishkes are the repository of all Jewish stress. A particularly troubling problem might "eat out your *kishkes*." Something that keeps you awake at night, *gridzjhen di kishkes* (gnaws at the guts). Bad news might feel like a "kick in the *kishkes*."

The *kishkes* are where secrets are kept: "She kept *shtumm* (quiet) for 35 years, then one day, she just spilled her *kishkes*."

It's where you aim in a fight: "If anyone ever tried to mug me, boy, I'd give him such a *chamalyah* (whallop) in the *kishkes*!"

And of course, it's the plumbing that needs to be Roto-Rootered, once in a while: "I haven't taken a shit in a week. Feels like my *kishkes* are filled with cement."

A gut feeling, however, is a *boykh-svoreh*, "a belly guess."

I feel…
Ikh fil…

> **like crap.**
> *nisht in gantzn.*
> Literally, "not whole."

> **bleeeeeeeeechhhh.**
> *blekhedikh. [BLEKH-a-dikh]*

> **icky.**
> *ibble-dikh.*
> This usually refers to nausea or an unspecified feeling of malaise.

> **chafed.**
> *ongehreebn.*

I need an ice pack for my headache.
*Ikh darf an **ayzzah** fur meyn kupveytik.*

My ankle is swollen.
*Meyn knekhl iz **geshvolln**. [Mine KNEKH'l iz gehSHVOL'n]*

ACHE)))
VEYTIK

Just add the word *veytik* onto a body part and you can complain about all of your ailments!

> I have [a]...
> *Ikh hob [a]...*
>
> > headache.
> > *kupveytik.*
> >
> > sore throat.
> > *haltsveytik.*
> >
> > earache.
> > *oyerveytik.*
> >
> > bellyache.
> > *boykhveytik.*

Damn! I burned my hand!
Gevalt! Ikh hob zikh farbrent di hant!

I cut my finger.
Ikh hob tseshnitn di finger. [tseh-SHNIT-n dee fihngeh]

It's bleeding!
Iz gayt blut!

Are you okay?
Tsi felt ikh eppis?

I'm so clumsy!
Oy, ikh bin a klutz!

I've broken my...
Ikh hob tsebrokhn [tseh-BRAWKH'n] meyn...

> **bone.**
> *bayn.*
>
> **elbow.**
> *elenboygn.*

hip.
lend.

skull.
sharbn.

fingernail.
naugl.

cyeglasses.
brilln.

Not so terrible!/It could have been worse!
Nisht geferlekh!
Literally, "not dangerous!" Vernacular for no harm done.

> You fell out of a tree and broke your arm? *Nisht geferlekh!* You're lucky you didn't crack your head open!

I have (a) …
Ikh hob (a) …

cold.
farkilung.

cough.
hist.
Histn means "to cough."

fever.
hitz.

overall lousy feeling/nausea.
nitgutkeit.
Literally, "not good-ness."

cramps.
krampfs.

hemorrhoids.
mehreedn.

ulcer.
mogn-geshvir.

diabetes.
tsuker-krenk.
Literally, "sugar sickness."

hernia.
killah.
A hernia truss is a *killah bendl*, which would make a great name for a Jewish wrestler.

dose of the clap.
feifer or trifer.

lice.
leiz.

I have heartburn.
Iz brent mir oyfen hartz.
Literally, "It burns in my heart." Note: *Hartzveytik* means "heartache," not "heartburn."

It's gonna give me a nervous breakdown!
*Az vilt gibn mir an **arbm-shvakh**.*

I ache all over.
Se tut mir vey yeder eyver.

·····Stop being such a hypochondriac!
A lung un leber oyf der noz!

A delusion is worse than a sickness.
An einredenish iz erger vi a krenk.

Another favorite sport among Jews is competitive hypochondria. A headache is never simply a headache, but the first symptom of a fatal brain tumor. The Yiddish expression for hypochondria, "A lung and a liver on the nose!" mocks the "sufferer" of imagined ridiculous maladies.

In a classic joke, a Frenchman, a German, and a Jew are trudging across the Sahara. The Frenchman says, "I'm so thirsty. I must have wine!" The German says, "I'm so thirsty. I must have beer!" The Jew cries, "*Oy*, I am so thirsty! I must have diabetes!"

If you're going to compete with the real players, you'd better know some good diseases:

To become infected with…
Onshtekn zakh mit…

pneumonia.
lungen-entsindung.
Or, what your mother is sure you will catch if you go outside without a hat.

dystentary.
disenteryeh.

malaria.
kadokhes.
Or any bout of fever marked by sweating and chills.

tuberculosis.
shvind-zukht.

whooping cough.
kookl-hist.
A rather funny name for an awful disease.

rickets.
ripkukhn.

And if you really want to be a drama queen, here's how to ratchet it up, one notch at a time…

Help!
Gevalt!
Also means "Emergency!" or "Oh God!"

My head is spinning…
Mir drayt zakh der kup…

I'm fainting…
Ikh bin challishn… [KHA-lish'n]

Call a nurse!
Ruf a krek-shvester!

Better call a doctor!
Besser ruf a doktor!

GO TAKE A SHIT!)))
GEH KAKN!

Eat shit and die!
Ess drek un shtarbn!

Shit on a stick
Drek oyf a sphendel
In other words, something worthless.

Shit with liver
Drek mit leber [LAY-ber]
What's worse than shit? Shit with liver, of course! It means, "less than nothing." As a kid, when my husband whined that he didn't like what his mother made for dinner, she'd say, "You know what you'll get to eat? *Drek mit leber!*"

Absolute crap
Chai kak serebrom [khaiy-kok]
Literally, "Eighteen pieces of silver-plated crap," usually shortened to simply *chai kak*. Also means, "worthless shit" or "absolutely nothing."

> She's divorcing me and she thinks she's gonna get half my money? You know what she'll get from me!? *Chai kak!*

Never mind! Call a specialist!
Mayleh! Ruf a spetzyalist!

Call an ambulance!
Shikt nakh an ambulanz!

I have to go to the hospital!
Ikh darf gayn in oshpitol!

It's getting dark before my eyes…
Iz vert mir finster in di oygen…

I'm a goner…
Ikh zayn farbay…

Too late…I'm dead already.
Tsu shpet…Ikh bin toyt shoyn.

·····Pee
Pishn

I gotta pee!
Ikh darf pishn!

I'm gonna pee in my pants!
Ikh geh pishn in meyn hoysn!

Which way to the can?
Avee iz dos vash-tsimmer?

He thinks his shit don't stink.
Er pisht mit boyml.
Literally, "He pees oil."

Piss
Pishakhs
Literally, "urine" but any nasty liquid unworthy of consumption.

They call this wine? Tastes like *pishakhs*!

·····Shit
Drek

Drek (or *drekht*) is a noun for "ca-ca." *Kakn* is the verb "to shit." While *kak* can also mean a big, steaming pile of literal or figurative crap, *drek* is more commonly used as the noun. Also used to describe poor-quality goods.

I gotta…
Ikh darf…

> **take a shit.**
> *gayn kakn.*
>
> **take a dump.**
> *doosn.*

Piece of shit
Shtik drek
Usually refers to a person or a thing.

I am constipated.
Ikh hob a shtayfer mogn.
Literally, "a tight stomach," i.e., tied in knots. Note: This does not mean "washboard abs!"

I'm all backed up.
Ikh bin farshtopung.

I have...
Ikh hob...

> **diarrhea.**
> *shilshul.*

> **the shits.**
> *a shittern mogn.*
> The runs. Ironically, *shittern* doesn't mean "shit." It means "pouring." *Mogn* is stomach or bowel.

·····Disgustingness
Khalusheskeit

He should fart in the sand.
Zol er fortzn in zamd.
A sarcastic way of saying, "He should rest in peace."

A pee without a fart, is like a wedding without a band. (Saying)
A pish on a fortz iz vi a chassineh [KHA-seh-nah] on a klezmer.

A nasty stink
Ipish

A horrifically putrid fart
Fortzn zoffer

> *Gevalt!* What the hell did you eat? That *fortzn zoffer* coulda knocked a buzzard off a shit wagon!

THERE'S A PRAYER FOR THAT?!)))
ES IZ A BRUKAH FUR YENER?!

Jews have prayers for everything. There are not only blessings before eating, but blessings for each food category (e.g., produce grown on trees, in the ground, on vines; bread, crackers, wine, water, etc). Jewish men have a special blessing in which they give thanks to God they were not born women whereas women give thanks for being created female. There are prayers said upon seeing a beautiful or strange-looking person, seeing a rainbow, upon hearing thunder, hearing good news or bad news, seeing a long lost friend, seeing the ocean for the first time in 30 days... Of course, there is even a blessing said after taking a piss or a shit. After all, you should be thankful to God Almighty that your bowels, and all your other tubes and ducts, are in fine working order, because we all know what happens when they aren't!

"Blessed are You, our God, Lord, Master of the Universe, who created mankind with wisdom and formed within him all manner of openings and cavities. It is obvious and known before the throne of glory that if even one of them were to be ruptured or blocked, it would be impossible to survive and to stand before You. Blessed are You, God, who heals all flesh and acts in wondrous ways."

Hand me a little **toilet paper**, would ya?
Gib mir a bisl asher yatzar papeer, ya?
Asher Yatzar is the key phrase of the prayer above (meaning "who created"), and is used in the slang expression for toilet paper.

To burp
Grepsn
And if the author of *Portnoy's Complaint* drank his seltzer too fast, you'd hear the....??? (Greps of Roth, of course!)

To vomit
Brekhn

It makes me wanna **barf**.
Ikh ken brekhn.
Literally, "I could vomit."

FARTING IN SYNAGOGUE)))
FORTZN IN SHUL

What happens if you're praying in synagogue, and are suddenly taken by an overwhelming urge to cut the cheese? Are there rules governing the religious etiquette for farting in temple? You betcha! It's all covered in the Talmud! (Yes, learned scholars actually debated over this!)

I'm paraphrasing here...

If you're *davening in shul* (praying in synagogue) and your sphincter can no longer contain the gaseous remnants of last night's *cholent* (bean stew), step back four cubits (roughly six to eight feet far enough so as not to asphyxiate any coworshippers with your heiny halitosis), float that fetid air biscuit as discreetly as possible, wait until the malodorous miasma of methane has dissipated, and recite the following prayer (in Hebrew):

> "Master of the Universe, You have created us with many openings and cavities. Our shame and our disgrace are open and known before You; shame and disgrace during our lifetime, worms and insects after death."

Then, step back to your place and resume the original prayer. And next time, easy on the *cholent*!

To hawk a loogie
Khrakn
Another great onomatopoeic word. You could hawk up a nice glob of phlegm just saying it.

To pick one's nose
Dloyben di noz

Sweaty
Farshvitzt

> I never worked so hard for an orgasm! Now I'm all *farshvitzt*.

To sweat
Shvitzn
A *shvitz* is the colloquial term for a steam bath.

> **It must be 110 degrees on this subway platform!
> I'm *shvitzing*!**

To sweat like a pig
Shvitzn vi a beeber
Literally, "to sweat like a beaver," because hey, pigs just ain't kosher!

To sneeze
Nisn

> #### A sneeze
> *A nis*

> #### Gesundheit!
> *Vahksin zols du tsu gezunt.*
> Literally, "May you grow to health."

> #### Bless you!
> *Vahksin zols du tsu leben.*
> Literally, "May you grow to life."

Zits
Kretzelakh

·····Tired
Fermahtert

To sleep
Shluffn

I need to take a nap.
Ikh darf khapn a drim.

I'm about to faint [from sheer exhaustion].
Ikh gai challishn bald avek. [KHAL-ish'n]

I'm a total wreck.
Ikh bin nisht mer vi a tsebrukhener sharbm.
The phrase translates to "I'm nothing more than a piece of a
broken old pot."

Weak/Thoroughly wiped out
Shvakh

To snore
Khroppen

To toss and turn
Varfn zikh
Varfn means to throw; *zikh* makes it reflexive. Thus, "to throw
oneself." You can *varf* a ball. *Varf* yourself in a shit fit. Or, *varf*
yourself in a fitful sleep.

CHAPTER 6

HORNY YIDDISH

YETZER-HOREH YIDDISH

Okay, so Yiddish isn't exactly the language of romance. Or sex. But it's not as if Yiddish speakers aren't having sex. Orthodox Jewish families don't have 14 children by parthenogenesis. It's just that Yiddish speakers tend to be a very modest lot. It's certainly not like English with our nine gazillion ways to say "fuck."

•••••Screwing
Shtupn

Shtup literally means "push" or "stuff." It's the most common, slangy way of saying "screw." It's far from polite, but because it's used so often in its literal sense, it's not a word that's going to get your mouth washed out with soap, either.

To copulate
Beheftn zakh

To sleep with me/you/him/her
Shluffn mit mir/du/im/ir

To bang me/you/him/her
Shmintzn mir/du/im/ir

To ravage/rape
Trenen
Literally, "to rip" or "tear" a seam; not a surprising euphemism, being that so many Jews were/are in the *shmata* biz. Quite rude when used in sexual contexts.

To fuck
Yentzn
Literally, "that." Originally a euphemism, it eventually became even dirtier than the word it replaced. This very rude term also means "to fuck over," i.e., to cheat or swindle.

> **He told me it was Ecstasy but it was only baby aspirin. That *momzer* (bastard) really *yentzed* me.**

He fucks like a wild animal.
Er yugt zakh vi a vildeh khayah.
Yugn zakh means "to mate," or "to rut" like an animal.

·····Licking and sucking
Lekhn un zoygn

Blow job
Shmeckel lekhn*

Do you spit or swallow?
Tzi du shpay oder shling?*

Lick my pussy.
Lekh meyn lokh.
Literally, "hole."

Muff diver
Lokh-lekher*
Literally, "hole licker."

Pussy eater
Knish nosher*

FLIRTING)))
KHAYNDLEN ZAKH

To chat up
Farfern

   chatted up
   hot farfeert

To bewitch/seduce
Farkishefn

Charm
Khayn

To charm
Makhn khayn
Literally, "making charm."

To clown around
Makhn zikh narish
Literally, "to make oneself the fool." A tactic to make oneself seem non-threatening and thus more adorable to the opposite sex.

Lust
Tayveh

Lustful
Tayvedik

Passion
Laydnshaft [lay-den-SHAFT]

Passionate
Laydnshaftlekh [lay-den-SHAFT-lekh]

I'm horny.
Ikh bin heis.
Literally, "I am hot."

Inept pussy eater
Koonilingus Kuni Lemel*
A *Kuni Lemel* is a clueless moron.

> He's got a big *shvantz* but he's a *koonilingus Kuni Lemel*.

Davening is praying, usually accompanied by a rhythmic, almost hypnotic rocking, back and forth (called *shuckling*).

A joke: Sarah marries Moishe, a very religious but sexually inexperienced young man. On their honeymoon night, he climbs on top of her, then just lays there like lox, without any clue what to do. Finally, totally frustrated, Sarah cries out, "*Daven*, Moishe! *Daven*!"

Carpet muncher
Peergah fresser
Literally, "pussy eater" (i.e., lesbian).

Hands of gold
Goldeneh hentz
Refers to the hands of a highly skilled artisan or craftsperson, but can also refer to the hands of someone who really knows how to diddle and fiddle the naughty bits, male or female.

> **She is the Queen of the Hand Jobs! I tell you, she has *goldeneh hentz*!**

•••••Kiss me!
Kish mir!

To kiss each other
Kishn zakh

Giving tongue
Gaibm loshen

Tonsil tickling
Tsing in tsingl

Swappin' spit
Shpinnen tsitses
Very foul. Literally, "spinning the fringes," referring to the ritual embellishments worn by religious men.

•••••Do you like it?
Gefelt es dir?

I like giving tongue.
*Gaibm loshen **gefelt mir.***
Literally, "To give tongue pleases me." Or, giving tongue does it for me.

I like big tits.
*Groys tsitskes **gefelt mir.***
Literally, "Big tits please me." Or, "Big tits do it for me."

I like....
Ikh veln keyn…
Literally, "X pleases me." Note the reverse construction.

I want...
Ikh veln keyn…

> #### to lick.
> *lekhn.*
>
> #### to spank.
> *opshmaysn.*

ORGASM)))
ORGAZM

Kummen means, literally "to come" but somehow, in *flagrante delicto*, "*Ikh kummmmmmmmmmmm...*" just doesn't have the same cathartic ring as "I'm cummmmmmmmmmmmmminggggg!"

If you insist on making Yiddish noises while climaxing (and honesty, I don't know why you would unless you want to "*shtup* your partner silly" because really, it's going to be difficult to keep a straight face), I suggest stringing together a few words from this list:

> Oh!
> *Oy!* Repeat as often as necessary.
>
> Jesus H. Christ!
> *Tatinue!*
> Literally, "Our Father!"
>
> Dear God!
> *Gutinue!*
>
> God in heaven!
> *Got in himmel!*
>
> Yeah, baby!
> *Ya, shaynah mama!* (said to a woman) / *Ya, tati!* (said to a man)
>
> That's it!
> *Azoy!*

to suck.
zoygn.

to bite.
beysn.

to tickle.
kitzln.
A tickle is a *kitzel*.

to slap.
patshn.
A slap is a *patsh*.

Screw me!
Shtup mir!

Holy crap!
Sheis!
Literally, "marble." Also used colloquially for "shit."

Oh yeah! That's gooooood!
Oy! Dos iz guuuuuut!

My balls are gonna explode!
Meyn beytsim zaynen gegangen oyfshisn.

Cum with me!
Kummen mit mir!

Now, baby, now!
Yetzt, tati/mami, yetzt!

I came...did you?
Ikh geplotzn...un du?

I love you!
Ikh hob dikh lieb!

Was it good for you?
Tsufreedn?
Literally, "Satisfied?"

to rub.
reybn. [Rl-bm]
Note: A "bn" combination is pronounced as "bm."

to cry out/scream.
shray'n.
A scream is a *geshray*.

> **He whipped his *shlong* out and from her
> *geshray*, you'd think an alien had burst out of
> his crotch.**

to stroke each other.
lontshen zikh.

to masturbate.
nekhvenin.

to cop a feel.
gayn mit di hant.
Literally, "to go with the hand"

to spurt.
shpritzn.

to feel up.
krikhn mit di hant.
Literally, "to crawl with the hand."

to shoot (one's load).
shisn.

to explode.
plotzn.

Beat me, hit me, spank me!
Klop mir, shlog mir, opgeshmays mir!*

I dig...
Ikh kleyb tayneg fun...
Literally, "I take pleasure from..."

working up a sexy sweat.
shvitzn und shpritzn.*
Literally "sweating and squirting," working hard to come.

We were going hot and heavy last night, *shvitzn un shpritzn.*

Do you want....?
Tsi viltstu...?

to spend the night
ibernekhtikn [ib-ber-NEKHT-tik-en]
Literally, "to overnight."

to go to the bedroom
gayn tsu der shluffzimmer

to play hide-the-kosher-salami
shpieln bahaltn der kasher salami

to get undressed
oyston zikh

to lie down
leygen zich

to play the clarinet (i.e., give a blow job)
shpieln der vursht*
Vursht literally means "sausage" but in musician's slang, it means "clarinet," so this is a triple entendre.

to play with yourself
shpieln zikh alayn

to make whoopee
tanzn di horehzontl hora*
Literally, "dance the horizontal hora."

to do the old push-push
makhn shtuppie-shtuppie*

a little belly button to belly button action
a bissel pupik tzu pupik shpieln*

my massive cock in your mouth
meyn shlong in deyn moyl

to have a threesome
hobn a Menasha Skulnik*
Skulnik was a great comic actor in the New York Yiddish theater. *Menasha* just *sounds* like a Yiddish-ized version of "ménage à" (as in "ménage à trois"), so this is what I've been calling it for years.

to 69
nayn un zekhtzik [ZEKHT-zik]

Not with you!
Nisht bi dir!

·····Vagina
Vagheena

While most Jews (and even plenty of gentiles) can give you half a dozen Yiddish words for "cock," words for its female counterpart are quite uncommon. Asking around among Yiddish speakers, the best anyone could come up with was *vagheena*, which is just a Yiddishized version of "vagina," or *mutersheyd*, which means "birth canal."

Legend (and by legend, I mean jokes) has it, Jewish women don't put out. No wonder they got such a bad rep! They didn't even have a name for their own va-jay-jays! A woman talking about a gynecological problem with her doctor would refer to her problem area as *dorten* (down there) or *meyn meiseh* (my story), or even *zakh* (thing).

I did manage to find a couple of "official" and some slang words for pussy, including the crude *shmunda*. Still, the list of words was woefully inadequate. To even out the balance sheets, I made up a few of my own because, hey, it's time we ladies had some good words for our naughty bits!

Va-jay-jay
Shmoonie ; Shmoondie
The child-friendly version of *shmunda*.

Juicy little hole
Zoftig lokhella*

Sweet pink button hole
Zeisseh rozeh knepllokh*

Vagina dentata
Vagheena mit tsayndlakh*
Literally, "vagina with teeth."

Naughty Bits
Erveh
From biblical Hebrew for "nakedeness," "undefended parts," or "shame," as in the story of Adam and Eve.

Fur Pie
Peergah
Literally, "*pierogi,*" from the Polish slang.

Pussy
Knish
Nobody titters at this word's double meaning. If you said, "I was hungry so I *noshed* on a *knish*," the listener would assume you snacked on a savory pastry. It's all about context.

> He *noshed* my *knish* for hours. I must have cum eight times!

Muffin
Hamentashen
Named for the jam or poppy seed–filled triangular pastries eaten on *Purim*. Like *knish*, above, it needs to be used in context for the meaning to be clear.

> **He put his *grogger* in my *hamentashen* and we did the whole *megillah*.**
> Or, he put his *Purim* noisemaker [dick] in my muffin and we did the whole long *Purim* story.

Twat
Fotz
From the German slang, *fotze*. Rare usage.

Cunt
Shmunda

Clit
Teigl
Teiglach is a holiday dessert consisting of a mound of small dough balls covered in a honey syrup. One honey-covered ball is a *teigl*, an apt name for a clit.

Love button
Lieb knop*

Cherry
Keersh

Hymen
Knipl
Literally, "nest egg," a woman's secret stash of savings, usually tied up in the corner of a hanky.

•••••Penis
Penis

Male member
Ayver
Literally, "limb."
This is the proper, "civilized" way to refer to one's winkie (i.e., when discussing that nasty itch with your doctor).

Winkie
Shmeckel
The child-friendly version of *shmuck*. It can imply a small or limp dick, or it can be just a familiar, funny way of referring to it.

Joystick
Grogger [GRAH-gur]
A noisemaker used on *Purim*, usually shaken and/or spun every time the evil Haman's name is mentioned, thus something waved around indiscriminately.

Pee-Pee
Mekki
Baby talk for *shmeckel*.

Cock
Shmuck
Literally, "jewel."

Weiner
Putz

Prick
Shvantz
Literally, "tail."

Weenie
Pitzeleh
Child-friendly version of *putz*. Also means "little squirt," an affectionate way of describing a young boy.

Massive cock
Shlong
Literally, "snake."

> **Ask not what my prick can do for you; ask what you can do for my prick.**
> *Frayg nit vos meyn **shvantz** ken ton fur dir; frayg vos du kenst ton far meyn **shvantz**.*

Stubby dick
Pimpl
Literally, "little pump." Ironically, this does not mean "pimple," although that's basically what it implies.

STIFF OR LIMP?)))
SHTAYF ODER SHLAF?

Hard-on
Kisheh ayver

Stiff
Shtayf

Hard and ready to go!
Der yetzer horeh iz bey im oyf!
Literally, "The evil urge is up!"

I've got a woody!
Ikh hob mir a klotz in hoysen!
Literally, "I got me a log in the pants!"

Bummer, I can't get it up.
Nebakh, ikh toyg nisht.
Literally, "I'm not fit for it."

Limp
Shlaf

Noodle dick
Lukhshen putz*

Dead snake
Toyt shlong*

Mr. Happy
Reb Fraylikh*

Little Moishe
Kleine Moishe*

Ding-dong
Klanger
Literally, "the clapper of a bell."

Uncircumsized (non-Jewish) penis
Kolbas
From the Polish, *kielbasa* (a kind of large pork sausage).

Uncircumcised cock (or *shiksa* pussy)
Trayf
Literally, "not kosher," thus the pussy or cock of a non-Jew,
especially during oral sex.

Balls
Beytzim
Hebrew for "eggs."

> ### If the grandmother had **balls**, she'd be my grandfather. (Saying)
> *Az di bubbeh volt gehat **beytzim** volt zi gevayn meyn zaydeh.*

A nice set of balls
Knaidlakh*
Literally, "matzoh balls," soup dumplings, about the right size and
weight.

Fuzzy balls
Farvisht beytzim

•••••Virgin or whore?
B'suleh oder nafka?

Virginity
B'suleh shaft

A virgin in her elbow
A b'suleh in elenboygn
In other words, the only place she's still a virgin.

Is she a virgin or not?
Bialy or bagel?*
In lieu of a bagel's hole, a *bialy* has an indentation, suggesting an
intact hymen.

Ho'
Zoyneh

He fucked that ho' and now she's pregnant.
Er hot gehshtupt yener zoyneh un atsind zi iz trogn.
Trogn literally means to carry or to wear. *Zi trogt* means she's carrying. Depending on context, she can be wearing a new hat, holding a bag of groceries, or packing a fetus.

Whore
Korva
Nice Jewish girls weren't…so this a Polish word, Yiddish by osmosis.

She was born a **whore**.
*Zi hot gevayn a **korva** in de moma's boykh.*
Literally, "She was a whore in her mother's belly."

Slut
Nafka

Big, fucking whore
Veltz korva
Literally, "world whore." She will fuck anyone, anytime, anywhere.

House of ill repute
Shandhoiz
Literally, a "shame house."

Brothel
Bordel ; Heizl

Pimp
Yentzer
Also means "fucker."

Pussy peddler
Peergah mekler

FOKH ME, BABY!)))

When you are heated or flushed (*darheytzn*), you need a *fokher*, a hand-held fan. (*Fokhn* is "to fan.") If you fan your mom, you're a mother*fokher*. If you're hot and want your friend to fan you, you could say, "*Fokh* me, baby! *Fokh* me hard!" If your friend doesn't want to fan you, he/she might say, "Go *fokh* yourself!"

·····Oh, behave!
Firn zikh!

Old perv
Alteh noyef
Dirty old man.

Womanizer
Veybernik

Lover
Kokhanik [ko-KHA-nik]/Kokhanikeh [ko-KHA-nik-keh]

Fetish
Kapurner yetzer horeh
Literally, "brazen evil inclination."

She's **frigid.**
*Zi is **kalt**.*
Literally, "cold."

Quit grabbing!
Khap nisht!
Literally, "Don't grab!" but colloquially, "Hey, slow down! Take it easy!"

CHAPTER 7

ANGRY YIDDISH

BROYGIS YIDDISH

For old-world Jews, hurling profanities is considered horrifyingly rude and somewhat sacrilegious. That's probably just as well, since if you're gonna call someone a motherfucker to his face, you'd better be prepared to defend yourself (or run).

There are few words that would get bleeped on Yiddish television…if there were such a thing. Generally speaking, Yiddish is not a profane language. There are no words for "motherfucker" or "son of a bitch." Yiddish speakers don't take the Lord's name in vain (so no "Goddamnits!" and certainly no "Jesus H. Christ!").

This is not to say Jews don't get angry. In fact, Jews tend to get angry about everything. We are exquisitely fine-tuned to injustice (of all kinds) and can sniff out bullshit like hound dogs.

·····Pissed off
Tsegridjeneh

Angry
Broygis
Also an ongoing conflict, on the outs with someone, not on speaking terms. Opposite of *sholem* (peace).

> **He walked in three hours late totally shit-faced. Hell, yeah, I'm *broygis*! But I'm such a softie, I'll probably make *sholem* with him tomorrow.**

To bother
Nudjen

> Stop *nudjing* me, already! I'll take out the garbage at the next commercial!

To pester
Mutshen

> He *mutshehs* me night and day. The man won't let me breathe!

To annoy
Gridjen

> You know what really *gridjes* me? Not that he broke up with me, but that he did it via text message!

To fight
Tsekrigen zikh

To hassle
Tsheppen
Obnoxious behavior that might prompt a backhanded *zetz* (whack).

A tempest in a teapot
A mikveh in a mayim akhroynim tepl
Literally, a "ritual bath in a soup pot."

SPLITTING HAIRS)))
PILPUL

Jews love to argue and we're very good at it. As the saying goes, "Two Jews, three opinions." This skill has been honed over millennia of Talmudic study, in which the most esoteric aspects of Jewish law or *halacha* are studied and discussed to death from every possible angle. It's this cultural tradition of scholarly legal analysis called *pilpul* that makes Jews such good lawyers.

Recently, it was discovered that tiny, microscopic crustaceans exist in New York City water. Being that crustaceans are *treyf* (not kosher), does that mean that city water is suddenly unkosher!? What about food made with NYC H2O? Is the New York City bagel, the very staff of life, no longer edible?! The *pilpul* went on for years. If there are 2,000 rabbis in NYC, there were at least 3,000 different opinions!

There is still no single agreed-upon resolution. Some are of the "what I don't know can't hurt me" school while many ultra-Orthodox rabbis deemed that even invisible *treyf* was *treyf* nonetheless, and advised that in order to keep a fully kosher home, one must install a special filter on the pipes to keep those pesky little critters out.

Perfect comeback
Trepsverter
Literally, "step words," that witty retort you wish you had thought of in the moment.

Grief
Tsuris
Also means problems, troubles. (Note: "Who's Got Bigger Tsuris" is another competitive sport in the Jewish Olympics.)

> **You think you've got *tsuris*? My daughter became a Scientologist. My wife is having an affair with the gardener. And I just lost ten grand in the stock market!**

·····Scram!
Gai avek!

Get lost!
Ver farblondjet! [far-BLON-dzhet]

Leave me alone!
Lɔz mikh tsu ru!

Hit the road!
Khap a gang!

Quit hassling me!
Tshepeh zikh nit tsu mir!

Stop yakking at me!
Hok mir nit kayn chainik!
Literally, "Don't bang on my tea kettle." This phrase is commonly used in Yinglish as, "Stop *hocking* me in *chainik*!"

Why are you talking my head off?
Vos hokst du mir in kup?

Quit bugging me!
Ferdray zikh oyf deyn kup!
Literally, "Go twist your own head around!" Emphasis on the *deyn* (your).

Get out!/Go, already!
Gai shoyn! Gai!
This can be used the same way "get out" is used in English, both in the literal sense and as in, "OMG, no way!"

Butt out!
Mish zikh nisht arayn!
Literally, "Don't mix yourself around!"

It's none of your business.
Es iz nit deyn gesheft.

Who says so?
A vooshtet geshraybn?
Literally, "Where is it written?"

Are you starting up again?
Du fangst shoyn on?

·····A little angrier
A bisl mir broygis

I spit on you!
Ikh feif oyf dir!
Literally, "I whistle on you!"

Drop dead!
Geharget zolstu veren!
Literally, "Killed, you should get!"

Go kill yourself!
Ver derharget!

HELL)))
DER ERD

While Jews believe in heaven (the spiritual equivalent to the all-you-can-eat buffet), we don't really subscribe to the whole fire and brimstone, red-horned Satan business. There are varying ideas about what happens after death. The closest notion to Christian hell is a year-long stay in *Gehenum* (also an actual valley just outside Jerusalem's walls, mentioned in the Bible as a place where pagans once sacrificed children). While in this purgatory, one ruminates and repents for his or her wrong-doings. Once the soul is purified, it ascends to heaven (sort of grad school for the *neshumeh*).

Der erd (often simply *drerd*) literally means "the ground" or "the mud" and in various expressions means "buried in the ground," i.e., dead. When one says *Gai mit deyn kup in drerd* ("Go stick your head in the mud") it doesn't mean "Go get your hair dirty." It means "Go to hell." (Also, *Gai in drerd arayn* literally means "Go in the ground.")

Fuck it!
Zol es brennen!
Literally, "It should burn!"

Rot in hell!
Ikh hob dikh in drerd!
Literally, "I'll have you in the ground!"

I hate him!
Ikh hob im feint!

Damn you!
A klog oyf deyn kup!
Literally, "A misery on your head!"

You ass!
Khamoyer du ainer!

Shut up!
Shtum zikh!

I'd like to give you a fever!
Ikh vel dir geben kodokhes!
In other words, "You ain't gonna get shit from me!"

I'll give you nothing!
Ikh vel dir geben bupkes!
Bupkes are goat turds. It's rarely used in the literal sense, and almost always used to mean "nothing" or "something of no value."

> **We've been dating for a month and you know what he got me for my birthday?** *Bupkes!*

Shut yer piehole!
Farmakh dos moyl!

Go explode!
Gai plotz!

Go swallow a fart!
Fortzdu in gurgul!
Literally, "Fart in (your) throat."

·····Nasty talk
Grobbeh rayd

Go fuck yourself.
Gai tren zikh.

Who do you think you're fucking with?
Vaymen barestu?
Baren means "to fornicate" but used in these phrases, it takes on the more taboo implication of "fuck."

Quit fucking around!
Bareh nit!

Don't fuck with me!
Bareh mikh nit!

Go bang your own head against a wall!
Gai shlug deyn kup en vant!

Fuck off!
Gai kakn ofn yahm!
Literally, "Go shit in the ocean!"

Don't be a jackass!
Zei nit kayn vayzoso!

A tragic end to you!
A finsteren sof!
Literally, "A dark ending!"

I shit on you!
Ikh kak oyf dir!

Shove it up your ass!
Zolstu shtupn in tookhis arayn!

Sticks and stones may break my bones...
Hob dir in arbel...
Literally, "I have you by the sleeve..."

•••••Angry in business
Broygis in geshaft

Put up or shut up!
Tookhis ofn tish!
Literally, "Ass on the table!"

> **Quit fucking around and sign the contract already.**
> ***Tookhis ofn tish!***

That's the way the cookie crumbles!
Zoy vert dos kukhl tzekrokhen!

What a disaster!
Oy, a brokh!

May everything you touch turn to shit!
A shvartz yohr!
Literally, "A black year!"

Any ass knows that!
Yaidr essl kent dos!

Don't get yourself all worked up!
Se brent nit!
Literally, "It's not burning!"

There...ya happy now?!
Tsufreedn?!
Literally, "Satisfied?!"

Something's fucked up.
Es gait nit!
Literally, "It's not going!" or "There's a serious glitch." From the
Yiddish *glitsh*, a slippery area.

SMARTS)))
SECHEL

Sechel [sekh'l] is a quality highly prized by Jews. Certainly education and wisdom are also valued, but *sechel* is more admired because it can't really be taught or learned. It's a native intelligence, a cleverness, a creative problem-solving ability or even a healthy dose of good old common sense.

> That new guy we're hired to reorganize the department has worked wonders! He's really got a lot of *sechel*.

> The first time it's cleverness; the second time it's charming; the third time you get a punch in the teeth.
> *Ayn mol a sechel; dos tsvaiteh mol khayn; dem dritten mol git men in di tsayn.*

Big deal!
Ayn kleinkeit!
Literally, "A smallness!"

Tough titties!
Az okh un vai!

What choice do I have?
A breyre hob ikh?

Why bother getting up alive?
Farshporn zol er oyf tsu shteyn?

He doesn't know what the fuck he's talking about!
Er redt in der velt arayn!
Literally, "He talks into the world!" In other words, he's speaking to the wind; let him yak…nobody's listening.

Don't mix business with pleasure.
Handelshaft iz kayn brudershaft.
Literally, "Business is not brotherhood." It also means, "Don't trust a relative in business."

I'm in deep doo-doo!
Bin ikh oyf gehakteh tsuris!
Literally, "I have some serious problems!"

You don't scare me!
Gai strasheh di vantzen!
Literally, "Go threaten the bedbugs!"

I don't give a rat's ass!
A daygeh hob ikh!

That's not gonna fly!
Nisht gefloygen!

The hell with him!
Ikh hob im in bod!
Literally, "I have him in the bath!" A euphemism for the toilet. Also means, "I don't give a shit."

I have him up my butt!
Ikh hob im in tookhis!
Said about an annoying pain in the ass.

I need it like I need a hole in the head!
Ikh darf es vi a lokh in kup!

A bunch of ignorant boors!
Prosteh menschen!

Go jump in the lake!
Gai feifen ofn yahm!
Literally, "Go whistle in the ocean."

Don't threaten me!
Strasheh mikh nit!

Obey me!
Folg mikh!

Give a pig a chair, he'll want to get on the table.
Az me lozt a chazzer [KHAZ-zer] aruf ofn bahnk, vil er ofn tish.

I sure told him off!
Ikh hob em arayngezoght in tatns tatn arayn!

Go take shit.
Gai in der klozet.
Literally, "Go in the closet." *Klozet* means "water closet" or WC, a more a polite way of telling someone to go take a shit.

I'm gonna make his life so fucking miserable!
Ikh'l em umgliklekh makhn!
Literally, "I'm going make him so unlucky!"

He may act all "holier than thou," but he's still a thief!
Er iz Gots gonif!
Literally, "He's God's thief!"

·····Now it's getting physical!
Verndik fizisheh!

Aside from maybe the Israeli Army, Jews aren't famous for their fighting skills. You're not likely to run into a shit-faced Jew in a bar, instigating brawls with strangers. It's hard to imagine two Hasids in a knock-down, drag-out fight. But certainly Jews have been the victims of violence, so yeah, we have words for it.

A light spank on the ass
A potsh in tookhis

A slap in the kisser
A frosk in pisk
A *frosk* is sharper than a *potsh*. A *potsh* is what you might give a small child; a *frosk* is what a girl might give a guy who tried to cop an unwelcome feel. A *pisk* is technically an animal's mouth and is often used in slang expressions.

A whallop
A chamalyah [kham-AL-yah]

Whack
Zetz
You can give someone a *zetz* or *zetz* someone, or even accidentally bang your head and give yourself a *zetz*. Sometimes used colloquially to mean "fuck."

> I was *zetzing* her pretty good, when her husband walked in…

A stab in the heart
A shtuken nisht in hartz
This is usually used dramatically and metaphorically.

> I put him through medical school, and now he's leaving me for that 22-year-old nurse he's been *shtupping*! *A shtuken nisht in hartz!*

·····Insults and name-calling
Zidlvort in di oygn

Sticks and stones may break your bones in English, but in Yiddish, insults are directed to a different body part. When someone disses you, they give you a *zidlvort in di oygn*, or "an abusive word in the eye."

Lame-o!
Gelaimter!
This literally means someone who is lame or crippled, but is colloquially used to describe anyone who's pathetically uncoordinated or totally inept.

Asshole!
Shmuck!

Jerkoff!
Putz!

Bastard!
Momzer!

Crazy bastard!
Meshuggeneh momzer!

MONEY)))
GELT

Wasted money
Aroisgevarfeneh gelt [uh-ROYS-geh-varf-en-uh gelt]

My money went down to hell!
In der erd meyn gelt!

Money on the table!
Gelt ofn tish!

The man is a piece of shit, but his money is good!
Der mensch iz treyf, ober zayn gelt iz kosher!
Literally, "The man is unkosher but his money is kosher."

Cash
Mezumen
From the Hebrew *mezuman*.

Sure, I trust you, but send cash!
Bist a botuakh, ober shik arayn mezumen!

ATM
Mezumenkeh
Who knew? There's actually a Yiddish word for this! (Not that anyone else is going to know what the hell you mean.)

In for a dime, in for a dollar.
Az men est chazzer, zol es shoyn rinen ibern moyl.
Literally, "If you're going to eat pork, eat until your mouth drips." This is the Yiddish equivalent of, "Jesus died for your sins so you might as well enjoy them."

Shoddy goods
Shlok
Crap made in China that falls apart five minutes after you get home.

Dumb ass!
Farshtopten kup!

You'll always be a clueless loser.
Du'st tomed blaybn a loiyutzlekh.

You spin around like a fart in a barrel.
Du drayst zihk arum vie a fortz in roosl.
In other words, you have no direction; you aimlessly and
purposelessly bounce around like a fart in a barrel.

A pig remains a pig.
A chazzer bleibt a chazzer. [KHAZ-zer]
While you could say this about somebody, it's pretty nasty when
you say it to someone's face. It's the equivalent of, "You'll never
change! You'll always be a low-life piece of shit!"

A fool remains a fool.
A nar bleibt a nar.
A bit less harsh.

A shame and a disgrace!
A shonda un a kharpeh!

A horror!
A shreklekheh zakh! [SHREK-lekh-eh]
Shrek (aka our favorite green ogre) literally means "terror" or "fear."
Shrekn means to frighten or horrify.

Big mouth!
Gembeh!

Low-down, worthless, good for nothing!
Niderrekhtiker kerl!

Hard-hearted SOB!
Kalta neshumeh!
Literally, "cold soul!"

Lights on, nobody home!
Dos hitl iz gut nor der kup iz tsu klein!
Literally, "The hat's okay, but the head's too small!"

Don't pee on my back and tell me that it's raining!
*Du kanst nikht oyf meinem rukhen pishen und mir zogn
klas es rehgen ist!*
Judge Judy's favorite line.

The public are **idiots!**
*Oylem **goylem**!*

A *goylem* (also *golem*) is a creature formed from mud and clay
that comes to life through magic spells and behaves like a robot,
with no will of its own. To call someone a *goylem* is to say they are
dumb as a lump of clay, helpless, unable to think for themselves.

If he were twice as smart, he'd be an **idiot.**
*Ven er iz tsvey mol azoy klug, volt er gevayn a **goylem**.*

Like lipstick on a pig.
Vi a chazzer oyringlekh.
Literally, "Like earrings on a pig."

If you put a fur hat on a pig, does that make him a rabbi?
Tu on a chazzer a shrayml, vet er vern rov?

CHAPTER 8

CURSY YIDDISH
BROKHISHE YIDDISH

As you learned in the Angry chapter, when Jews get pissed off, they fight with words—or patiently wait to get revenge in more calculated, intellectual, and less-confrontational ways. This is what I call "Jew-Jitzu"—the fine art of bringing an enemy to tears, with devastating honesty or just the right turn of phrase.

As one smart-ass Yid once said, *Es shit zikh fun im khokhmes vi fun a tsig bobkes*. Translation: "Witticisms pour out form him like turds from a goat." Insulting someone in Yiddish is a far more intellectual pursuit than a mere battle of hurling profanities. To curse someone is literally to put a curse on them; to curse someone is to wish them uncomfortable, painful, and perhaps ironic suffering, although not death. (Who needs the guilt or karmic responsibility for somebody's death?) Thus, kidney stones, toothaches, a tapeworm in the *kishkes*, some nice pustulating sores? All fair game. Cancer, heart attacks, anthrax? Off limits.

A PROPER CURSE)))
A RIKHTEKEH BROKH

A good curse is pure creative genius, like the plot of a short film. It requires imagination and a strong sense of satire. The best curses begin innocently enough, often starting out as a blessing, lulling the recipient into a feeling of false security...then WHAM! The whole thing twists around into wishes of horrific disaster or intolerable pain.

Yiddish curses were the "Yo Mama!" competitions of their day. The funnier, nastier, more outlandish, and disgusting, the better. There were many "classics" that were used again and again, and which are included in this chapter. For creative types, however, making up original curses could be a cathartic challenge.

Now that you have a good sense of what constitutes a proper Yiddish-style curse, you can try making up some of your own, in English or Yinglish.

•••••Sickness and physical discomfort
Krenkheit un veytik

Next time somebody pisses you off, instead of stooping to their level and calling them a jackass, why not say something classy like:

You should get...
Se zol dir...

a stomach cramp.
grihmen in boykh.

a fire in your liver.
a fyer in deyn leber. [LAY ber]

a sharp pain in your guts.
a shnaydenish dir in di kishkes.

an abscess on your head.
an geshvir dir in kup.

a fever in your bones.
a kadokhes dir in di beyner.
Note: *Kadokhes* is more than just a temporary uptick in body temp. It implies a more serious illness often translated as "malaria," "recurrent fever," or "delirium."

Beets should grow out of your belly button, and you should piss borsht.
Zoln dir vaksn boorekes fun pupik in zolst pishen mit borsht.

Your guts should be pulled out of your belly and wrapped around your neck!
Aroysshlepn [a-ROYZ-shlep'n] zol men dir di kishkes fun boykh un arumviklen deyn haldz!

May all your teeth fall out except one, and in that one, you should have a terrible toothache.
Alleh tseyen zoln dir aroisfaln, nor eyner zol dir blaybn—oyf tsonveytik.

You should have a seizure!
A nikhpe zol dikh khapn!

He should get so sick that he coughs up his mother's milk.
Oyskrenkn zol er dos mamehs milkh.

May your bones be broken as often as the Ten Commandments!
Zoln deyn beyner zikh brekhn azoy oft vi di Aseres-Hadibres.

·····Eating and indigestion
Essen un boykhveytik

Some believe that all (or at least most) illness is psychosomatic. Well, then, what better way to create intestinal rumbling in an enemy than with a cleverly planted posthypnotic suggestion?

You should have thunder in your belly and lightning in your pants!
Es zol dir dunern in boykh un blitsn in di hoyzn!

May you have such rumbling in your stomach, it will sound like a [*Purim*] noisemaker.
Es zol dir dunern in boykh, vestu meyen az s'iz a Haman klaper.

A cramp in his flesh and his guts!
A krampf im in layb un in di kishkes!

You should swell up to the size of a mountain!
Zolst geshvollen veren vi a barg!

May you be invited to a fancy state dinner by the governor and burp in his face.
Meh zol din aynlaydn tsum gubernator oyf a seder in du zolst im gebn a greps in punim arayn.

You should have the fattest goose, but no teeth; the best wine, but no sense of taste; and the hottest wife, but can't get it up.
Zolst hobn di sameh gandtz, nor kit kayn tsayner; di besteh vayn nor kit kayn khushtem; di sensteh vayb, nor nit kayn zehrut.

May you eat chopped liver with onions, shmaltz herring, chicken soup with dumplings, baked carp with horseradish, vegetable stew...every day—and may you choke on every bite!
Essn zolstu gehakteh leber mit tsibeles, shmaltz hering, yoykh mit knaydlekh, karp mit khreyn, tsimes... yedn tog— un zolst zikh mit yedn bis dershtikn!

May you run to the toilet every three minutes or every three months!
Lofyn zolstu in bet-hakisay yeder dri minut oder yeder dri khoydeshim!

He should shit blood and pus.
Er zol kakn mit blit un mit ayter.

You should fall into an outhouse during an epidemic of diarrhea!
Er zol faln ayn an optret beshis an epidemia fun shilshul.

You should go to hell and bake bagels!
Er zol lign in drerd un bakn beygl!

Hang yourself with a sugar rope and you'll have a sweet death.
Heng dikh oyf a tsikershtrikl vestu hobn a ziessen toyt.

You should swallow a trolley car and shit transfers!
Zoltstu essn a trolley car un kakn transfers!

•••••Disaster and destruction
Umglik un churbn

While physical suffering is always a nice thing to wish on an enemy, sometimes, for variety, it's nice to wish them a more general kind of misery.

A blessing for success...on your pile of troubles!
A mazel-brukheh oyf deyn hoyfen tsuris!

May calamity strike you and your whole famn damily!
A brod oyf dir un oyf deyn!

A lunatic should be crossed off the register of crazies and you should be inscribed in his place!
A mishuggener zol men oysshraybn un dikh araynshraybn!

Onions should grow from your belly button!
Zol vaksen tsibbelis fun pupik!

You should grow like an onion, with your head in the ground!
Zolst vaksn vi a tsibbele mitn kup in drerd!

May your life be filled with disaster!
A brokh tsu deyn lebn.

Better your mother had birthed a stone than you!
Beser volt oyf deyn ort a shteyn arayn.

I should see you on one leg and you should see me with one eye!
Ikh zol dikh zayn oyf ayn fus, un du men mit ayn oyg.

Your enemies should sprain their ankles…dancing on your grave!
Zoln deyn shunim oyslenken zeyereh fim ven zay veln tanzn oyf deyn keyver!

You should be as tormented in death as I am in life!
Zolst zid azoy matern mint toyt vi in mater zid!

May every nightmare fill your head.
Alleh bayz khlolomet tsu deyn kup.
Literally, "All bad dreams in your head."

·····Misfortune on you!
Eyn umglik oyf dir!

Jews have it hard enough in this world, thank you very much. Even a wish for a bit more *tsuris* (grief) is sometimes all that's needed to tip the balance from "just hanging on" to abject misery.

You should become so rich that your widow's husband won't have to worry about earning a living.
Zolstu veren azoy raykh az deyn almonehs mahn zol zikh kayn mol nit zorgn vegn parnoseh.

A HORRIBLE DEATH!)))
A MEESEH MESHINA!

This is the most serious curse of all and not one to be taken lightly. It was reserved for the worst anti-Semitic tormentors of the Jews. When a gang of drunken Ukrainians laughingly knocked a Jew into the mud for fun; when Russian soldiers stormed into a *shtetl* (small town), taking and destroying everything they wanted, this was the curse. It was used for Nazis and the KKK; for the Czar who conscripted young Jewish boys into his army for life, for any bully who abused people simply because they were Jewish.

In the old world, Jews were required to "know their place." Any attempt to fight back against the rampant abuse was met with serious repercussions, not just for themselves, but for their entire community. This curse was their only "recourse." It was never used lightly or casually, and almost never against another Jew.

It means, "May you die a cruel death of unimaginable suffering, a thousand times worse than what you are inflicting on me now, far away from your family and friends, in the mud, without any human dignity, like the animal you are." For a pious Jew, who believes God hears his prayers, this curse is serious business.

Many etymologists believe that "sheeny" (disparaging slang for a Jew) is derived from this expression. Because the curse was usually mumbled under the breath, the tormentors only heard the end, "sheena," which eventually became, "sheeny," another way to mock Jews.

He should give it all away to doctors.
Oyf doktoyrim zol er dos avekgeybn.
Or, he should have to spend all his money on doctors.

A hundred houses may he have, and in every house a hundred rooms, and in every room 20 beds, and a delirious fever should toss him from bed to bed.
Hindert hayzer zol er hobn, in yeder hoyz a hindert tsimern, in yeder tsimer tsvonsik betn un kadokhes zol im varfn fineyn bet in der tsveyter.

One misfortune isn't enough for him.
Ayn imglik is fur im veynik.

Ten ships of gold should be his and all that money should only make him sick.
Tsen shifn mit gold zol er farmorgn, un dos gantzeh gelt zol er farkrenkn.

He should have a large store, and whatever people ask for he shouldn't have, and what he does have, nobody should ask for.
A groys gesheft zol er hobn mit shroyre, vos er hot, zol men bay im nit fregn, un vos men fregt zol er nisht hobn.

·····Curses with animals
Brokhs mit behaymehs

May your soul enter a cat, and a dog should bite it!
Deyn neshumeh zol arayngeyn in katz, un a hund zol er a bis tun.

Worms should make a wedding in your stomach and invite all their relatives—from Yehupetz to Slabodka!
Zoltz verrum praven a khassanah in deyn boykh un aynlaydn alle zayereh kroyvim—fun Yehupetz biz Slabodka!
Yehupetz is author Sholem Aleichem's fictional version of Kiev; Slabodka is a shared name of several small settlements in the far reaches of eastern Europe. Colloquially, "far and wide."

You should be turned into a blintz and the cat should snatch you!
Veren zol fun dir blintshik, un di katz dikh khopn!

May you be so articulate that only the cat can understand you.
Zolst azoy zayn redn az nor di katz zoln dir farshtayn.

Leeches should suck him dry!
Trinken zoln im piavkehs!

·····A plague on them!
A kholere oyf zay!

A Yiddish proverb says, "A curse is not a telegram; it doesn't arrive so quickly." A slow-acting curse gives you time to make your getaway. Who cares if your boss or your landlord is making your life miserable? They're living on borrowed time! You can sit back, Zen-like, and gloat as you wait for your Jewdoo to work its magic.

He should have Pharaoh's plagues tossed in with Job's leprosy.
Er zol hobn paroys makehs bashotn mit oybes kretz.

Yellow and green, he should become!
Fargelt un fargrint zol er vern!

A disease should afflict his gums!
A krenk zol im arayn in di yoslis.

He should go crazy and run around through the streets.
Mishuggeh zol er vern un arumloyfn ibber di gasn.

God should strike him with the best of the ten plagues.
Gut zol oyf im onshikn fin di tsen makehs di besteh.

A small child should be named after him.
A klein kihnd zol nokh im heysn.
Ashkenazim (i.e., Yiddish-speaking Jews) name their children after the dead to honor them. Wishing that a child be named after someone living is to wish that person dead.

I should live long enough to bury him.
Vi tsu derleb ikh im shoyn tsu bagrobn.

God should give him everything his heart desires, but he should be a cripple and not be able to use his tongue.
Got zol gebn, er zol hobn altsding vos zayn harts glist, nor er zol zayn gelaymt oyf alleh ayvers un nit kenen rirn mit der tsung.

He should turn into a chandelier, by day to hang and by night to burn.
Migulgl zol er vern in a henglayhter, by tog zol er hengen, un bay nakht zol er brenen.

All the problems I have in my heart, he should have in his head.
Alleh tsuris vos ikh hob oyf meyn hartzn, zoln oysgeyn tsu zayn kup.

A beautiful, purified plague on them.
A shaynem, raynem kapore oyf zey.
Note the rhyme in Yiddish.

Black sorrow is all his mother should see of him.
Finstere leyd zol nor di mama oyf im zen.

God should bless him with three people: One should grab him, the second should stab him, and the third should hide him.
Got zol im bentshn mit dray menschen: Eyner zol im haltn, der tsveyter zol im shpaltn, un der driter zol im ba'haltn.
Note the rhyme in Yiddish.

A venereal disease should eat his flesh.
Fransn zol essn zayn layb.

He should acquire a wooden tongue.
A holtsener tsung zol er bakumn.

He should have lots of troubles.
Er zol zayn tsoor.

THE YIDDISH EXORCIST)))
DER DYBBUK

Spiritual possession is rare in Judaism, but it does happen (at least, that's what they say). Unlike a Catholic possession, these are not demonic spirits. Rather, they are the souls of human beings who've passed on without dealing with some serious shit here on Earth. These spirits are called *dybbuks* or *dybbukim*. They attach themselves to a living human being like spiritual Velcro (*dybbuk* comes from the Hebrew for attachment or clinging) in order to finally put to rest whatever they left unfinished.

Should you worry that a *dybbuk* will slip into your body and command you to do its bidding? Probably not. The theory is that they only enter a human whose soul and body is already "broken apart," (i.e., severely depressed, schizophrenic, etc.). The spirit enters someone who possesses similar thoughts or goals but lacks the will to act on them. The unstable person, for instance, may harbor fantasies of starting fires but wouldn't actually do it. The pyromaniacal *dybbuk*, however, steps in and controls the human being. Before you know it, he's burnin' down the house.

Jews do perform exorcisms, but only in the presence of a *minyan* (a prayer quorum of ten men). Instead of driving a demon from a human body, the goal is to heal both souls simultaneously so they can both go their merry (and separate) ways.

Dybbukim aren't always malevolent. They can function as a kind of guardian angel, protecting the wounded soul of the host. The spirit has already "been there, done that" and comes to support and help the host persevere and heal. Once the crisis is past, these *dybbukim* usually leave on their own accord.

Let him suffer and remember.
Zol er krenken un gedenken.
In other words, he should be consumed by the memory of all the things he's done to deserve his current bad karma. Note the rhyme in Yiddish.

·····A curse on you!
A brokh tsu dir!

As I said, wishing serious ill on someone is not a matter to be taken lightly. Sometimes, however, you just need an extra-strength curse, say for Nazis, marauding Cossacks, or the KKK.

A pestilence should strike you!
A mageyfeh zol oyf dir kumen!

May suffering consume you!
Oysgehfleekt [OYS-geh-fleekt] zolstu vern!

May you never become old.
Nit derlebn zolstu altehtsu vern.
In other words, you should die young.

Your legs should be chopped off from under you!
Di fim zoln dir untergehakt vern.

May a fire burn you up!
A fyer zol did farbrenen!

Your bones should rot in hell!
Deyn bayner zoln foylen in gehenum!

You should fall and never get up again.
Faln zolstu nit oyfshteyn.

You should get fucked in the ass by a drunken Cossack with cholera.
Zolst du zayn geshtupt in tookhis durekh a shikker Cossack mit kholeirya.

All the malevolent spirits of mothers-in-law, from the time of King Solomon, should go into your mother-in-law and she should nag you incessantly.
Zollen zitsn alle dybbuken fun shvigger fun Shloimeh ha-Melekh in deyneh shvigger, un zollen zei dikh fur ein mol totshen.

·····Yiddish-inspired cursing in English
Yiddishe-nosakh fur klole in Anglish

Most Yiddish curses were created centuries ago. While many included in this chapter retain their humor even today, few reflect 21st century realities.

Using the basic format of the old-style Yiddish curse, here are a few riffs on the old formula for contemporary consumption:

> May your smart phone accidentally forward your girlfriend's naughty sexts to your wife.

> Upon your return flight from your mother-in-law's place in Florida, may you be subjected to an anal probe.

> May all your hair fall out—except on your *tookhis,* which you'll comb up your back and over your bald pate into a ridiculous Donald Trump pompadour.

> May that awesome cougar from Match.com you're trying to hook up with turn out to be your tenth grade English teacher!

> May your embarrassing bar mitzvah video go viral.

> May every ex-boyfriend you Google be wildly successful, still hot, and happily married to someone much younger than you.

> May you develop the unibrow to end all unibrows.

CHAPTER 9

HUNGRY YIDDISH
HUNGERDIK YIDDISH

Conservatively speaking, 80 percent of Jewish life revolves around food. Always on our mind are questions like, "When do we eat?" "What did you eat?" "When are we eating again?" and "Maybe we should eat a little something now so we don't faint before the meal?" This undoubtedly comes from millennia of uncertainty. Since you never know when you'll be driven from your home, it's always best to eat when food is available.

·····Eat, pray, and be a decent human being!
Ess, bench, un sei a mensch!

Snack
Nosh (both a verb and a noun)

> I love *noshing* on Costco samples.

> Let's have a little *nosh* before we go out.

To eat
Essen

> *Oy,* just look at you! So thin! *Ess, ess!*

FOOD BLESSINGS)))
MOTZI

Jews have several specific blessings for each type of food, depending whether a food is the fruit of "the earth," "the vine," "the tree," "the ground," etc. There are different prayers for full meals (which require a ritual washing of the hands) versus for snacks (which you can theoretically eat with *shmutzik* (dirty) hands).

The word *motzi [MOW-tsee]* derives from a word within the prayer over bread, known in shorthand as HaMotzi, from the Hebrew "to bring forth."

To snarf
Fressen
To devour food like a wild animal.

> It took me two hours to cook dinner and he *fressed* it all up in five minutes!

To grab
Khopn

> Let's *khop* a *nosh* before the movie.

I'm starving!
I'm challishing! [KHAL-lish]
Literally, "weak for..." or "craving in a big way." You most often hear it in relation to hunger, the way we might say, in English, with exaggeration, "I'm starrrvvvving!" It would never describe famished children in Africa, although you could *challish* for other drool-worthy things such as an awesome handbag or George Clooney.

To explode
Plotzn
One can *plotz* from overeating, good news, bad news, and even overexcitement.

> If I eat one more bite, I'm going to *plotz*!

> Oh my Gawd! When I saw Barbra Streisand at that bar mitzvah last week, I almost *plotzed*!

Don't bother me when I'm eating!
Ven ikh ess, kh'ob ikh alles in drerd!
Essentially, "When I'm eating, everyone else can drop dead!"

Breafast
Frishik

Dinner
Mitahg
Traditionally, the main meal was taken at midday, with a light supper in the evening. In America, that tradition was reversed. "Lunch" as we know it, is not a Yiddish concept, and so uses the English word.

Supper
Vehkhehreh

Appetizers
Forshpeyz
The mandatory *nosh* to keep you from *challishing* before dinner.

Leftovers
Ibbergehblibbehness [IB-ber-geh-BLIB-er-ness]
And leftover blintzes would *be ibbergehblibbeneh blintzes*, of course!

•••••Kosher
Kashrus

Jewish law divides foods into four categories: dairy, meat, neutral foods, and that which is unkosher (*treyf*). It's always forbidden to mix milk with meat, a law based on a passage in the Bible: "Thou shall not seethe a kid in its mother's milk." There are many other reasons why various foods, animals, or even animal parts from otherwise kosher animals may be unkosher, but you'd have to be a Talmudic scholar to understand them all.

The kosher "police"
Mashgiakh
The rabbi or learned supervisor (male or female) who certifies everything as kosher in restaurants, hotels, catering halls, food processing plants, etc.

Hardcore kosher
Glatt
Literally, "smooth." For meat to be kosher, it must be defect-free and from certain parts of a kosher animal slaughtered according to Jewish law. The term *glatt*, which once was used to refer to smooth, disease-free lungs, now speaks of a stricter level of *kashrus* in all things. It also refers to someone who keeps super-strictly kosher (often said in a derogatory way).

Dairy
Milkhig (noun) ; milkhadik (adjective)
Milk, cheese, or any kind of dairy food.

AT ISRAELI CUSTOMS)))
BI TSAULAHMT IN YISROEL

Yaakov immigrates to Israel by boat, bringing with him seven refrigerators. Once he arrives in Haifa, he is stopped at the port by a customs official.

"Sir, you are allowed to bring in only household appliances for your own personal use."

"These are for my own personal use," Yaakov explains. "I'm Orthodox, so I need one for *milkhig*, one for *fleishig*, and one for *parve*."

"Fine," says the official. "But that's only three. It still doesn't explain seven."

"You're forgetting Passover," says Yaakov. "I also need *milkhig, fleishig,* and *parve* for Pesach."

"Okay. So now we're up to six. It still doesn't add up to seven," says the customs officer.

Yaakov says, "And, *nu*, what if once in a while I want to eat a little *treyf*?"

Meat
Fleish
Certain parts of beef, lamb, and fowl are kosher when the animal is properly and humanely slaughtered by a *shochet [SHOKHet]*, a religious Jew licensed and trained to assure the killing is swift and painless, and the meat is drained of all blood.

Meaty
Fleishig / Fleishidik

Dietetically neutral
Parve
Often also spelled *pareve*. The food equivalent of Switzerland. Neither milk nor meat, *parve* foods can be eaten with dairy or with meat. This includes fruit, vegetables, nuts, most non-dairy

beverages, and many other foods, including kosher fish with gills and scales.

Unkosher
Treyf
Any food that is not kosher by its very nature (i.e., pork or shrimp, improperly slaughtered meat) or because it combines meat and dairy. A hamburger might be made of 100 percent kosher beef, but a cheeseburger is always *treyf*. (Behavior, such as adultery, can also be *treyf*.)

Kosher for Passover
Kasher fer Pesach
During the week of Passover (*Pesach*) it is forbidden to eat foods containing leavening. Normal flour is prohibited but *matzoh* meal is allowed. Bread, everyday cakes, cookies, crackers, beer, and many other items are off limits. This does not mean Passover food is dietetic or carb-free! (As if!) Jews have created a vast array of holiday options, including *kugel*, macaroons, flourless chocolate cakes, sponge and nut cakes, candy, and more.

Food that is unkosher for Passover
Khummitz
Religious Jews sometimes maintain separate refrigerators, ovens, sinks, and dishwashers to keep milk and meat products (and dishes) apart. The really religious, who can afford it, sometimes have an entirely separate kitchen strictly for Passover use, thus assuring that no bits of *khummitz* get into their food during the holy week.

·····Tasty!
Batampt!

Ask a Yid for the best dish he or she ever ate, and they'll tell you with certainty the where, when, and what. "*Oy*, that *kishke* was the best I ever ate! I can still taste it 30 years later!"

Delish!
Geshmak!

Melts in your mouth!
Tsegayt zikh in moyl!

Finger-lickin' good!
Meh ken lekhen di finger!
Literally, "One can lick the finger!"

A little more of the noodle pudding, please
Nawkh a bissel *fun der kugel, zayt azoy gut.*

Thanks! That's enough!
A dank! ***Dos is genug!***

This is disgusting!
*Dos iz **khalushesdik**! [khal-OO-shus-dik]*

May it give you indigestion!
*Zol es dir **farshatn**!*

Choke on it!
Ver dershlikt!

·····To cook
Kukhn

No-recipe cooking
Shitterayn [SHIT-er-ayn]
A little of this, a little of that…have a taste and add a bit more. No measuring, no writing down…all by instinct and memory.

> **My grandmother was a great cook, but she always cooked by *shitterayn*; when she died, all her recipes went with her.**

To dabble
Patschki [POTCH-key]
To throw things together somewhat creatively, though not necessarily with ideal results. To experiment, play around with (not only with food).

This is delicious! Can I have the recipe?

  Oh, no recipe. I was just *patshki*-ing around in
  the kitchen.

Hodgepodge
Kockapootzi ; Kockapitshi
A mish-mosh mash-up of different things (food, styles,
design) that don't usually go together. (Not to be confused
with *caccapuzzi*, which is Italian baby talk for "You smell like
poo-poo.")

•••••Eat! Eat!
Ess! Ess!

Jewish food is, generally speaking, "poor people food." In the
Old Country, delicacies were, by necessity, contrived from the
humblest of ingredients, and of course, it all had to be kosher.
Even with these limitations, Jewish soul food is usually pretty
darn delish. What's not to like about a crispy *latke* (potato

pancake) or creamy *blintz* (cheese-filled crêpe?) So, *nu…Ess, ess! Es geshmak!* (Eat, eat! It's delish!)

Shmaltz
Chicken fat
What butter is to French cuisine, *shmaltz* is to Yiddish cooking. It gives many dishes their distinctive flavor and assures that Jews have cholesterol levels hovering around Lou Gehrig's batting average. *Shmaltzy* refers to something overdone or overly sentimental, such as a weepy movie, book, or theatrical production that requires you to use an entire box of Kleenex.

Tsibelis
Onions
Jewish cooking is not famous for subtly of flavor. It's pretty "one note." And that one note is fried onions. Without them, many savory dishes would be tasteless.

Yoykh
Chicken soup
Aka Jewish penicillin.

with noodles
mit lukshen

with ravioli
mit kreplach
Filled with a purée of meat and onions sautéed in *shmaltz*.

with *matzoh* balls (dumplings)
mit k'naidel
As Marilyn Monroe asked when she went to dinner at Arthur Miller's parents' home, "Do you Jews eat any other part of the *matzoh*?"

Matzoh
Passover "crackers," aka "The Bread of Affliction" (as it is called in the Passover story), and if you've ever eaten a lot of *matzoh*, you know why they call it that. This unleavened bread looks like perforated cardboard and tastes about the same. It's also more constipating than drinking cement! After eight days of *matzoh*, *matzoh* balls, *matzoh breis*, etcetera, etcetera, you

BOILED VS. BAKED)))
OPGEKOKHT VS. GEHBAKHT

Ah, the bagel! That delicious circle of leaden dough! Mickey Katz, hilarious Jewish singer and songwriter, called them "doughnuts dipped in cement." What gives them their distinctive heft, sheen, and taste is that they are boiled before being baked.

Traditional bagel flavors are plain, onion, garlic, poppy seed, sesame seed, salt, everything (all of the above), and raisin. Nowadays, you see all kinds of crazy variations including, chocolate chip, asiago, sun-dried tomato, and *oy gevalt*, bacon!

The *bialy* is the bagel's idiot cousin. A round, yeasty roll, similar to a bagel...but baked without boiling, and thus less dense. In lieu of the bagel's hole, the bialy boasts a depression in its center, usually filled with chopped onions and seeds before baking.

Order your bagel or *bialy* with...

> cream cheese
> *krem kez*
> More commonly, a *shmear*, now universal vernacular for a smear of cream cheese.
>
> smoked salmon
> *loks*
>
> butter
> *putehr*
>
> white fish
> *veisehr fish*

feel as if you're never going to be able to take a shit again. Undoubtedly, this is what Moses meant when he said "Let my people go!"

Kasha
Buckwheat groats. Back in Russia, groats were fed to horses. Jews were looked down upon for eating such lowly stuff. But hmmm, with some fried onions and *varnishkes* (bow tie pasta), oh baby! Dat's good eats!

Gribennes [GRIB-be-ness]
The kosher equivalent of (pardon the expression) fried pork rinds made instead with fried chicken skin.

Ptsha
An Old Country delicacy: cow, chicken, or duck feet in jelly. I've never heard of this being served anywhere and have never known anyone who actually eats it (thank God!).

Fliegl
The wing: an oft fought-over part of the chicken or turkey.

Borsht
Beet soup. When something is "dirt cheap," it's *billig vi borsht*, literally, "cheap as borsht."

Gehokteh leber [geh-HOK-teh lay-ber]
Chopped liver. Commonly used sarcastically to imply something worthless.

> **He must have *shtupped* every girl in my sorority except me. What am I? *Gehokteh leber?***

Gefilte fish
Carp, ground with *matzoh* meal, formed into balls or bullet-shaped patties; it's usually served with fresh *khrain* (horseradish). It's an acquired taste, which frankly, many never acquire.

Lukshen
Noodles

Kugel
A baked "pudding" with the consistency of a frittata or casserole. *Kugel* can be sweet or savory, made with vegetables, noodles, or, for Passover, *farfel*. My favorite supper as a kid was a sweet *lukshen kugel* with farmer cheese and raisins.

Farfel
Basically, *matzoh* confetti, *farfel* is often used as a base for *kugels* or for *matzoh brei*, a breakfast egg dish eaten during Passover. Basically, it's *matzoh* French-toast, usually sprinkled with cinnamon sugar or drizzled with syrup.

Charoset (or Charosis) [KHAR-o-set]
A sweet combination of roughly equal portions of chopped apples and walnuts doused with sweet wine. An important ritual dish served at the Passover seder, it represents the mortar used to build the pyramids.

Challah [KHAL-kah]
Egg bread usually served for Sabbath or holiday dinners. Makes *the* best French toast. Ever. Soak a nice thick slice in some beaten egg, a splash of *milkh*, dash of vanilla, sprinkle of cinnamon, and maybe a few grates of fresh nutmeg. Lightly fry in butter on both sides, until just golden brown. Top with powdered sugar or syrup. Mmm… perfection.

Latkes
Potato pancakes. Traditional *Chanukah* food…served with apple sauce or sour cream. These days, a lot of people make *latkes* with a food processor. That's cheating! They're not REAL *latkes* unless they have a bit of knuckle skin from hand-grating potatoes and salt from onion-chopping tears.

Tsimmis
A traditional slow-cooked stew of carrots, sweet potatoes, prunes, and raisins. Sometimes also made with beef. Colloquially, it's used the way "big stew" means "big fuss" in English.

> **So, you both wore the same dress to the party! Stop making a *tsimmis* about it.**

Cholent
A meat and bean stew traditionally served for *Shabbos* lunch. Because it's forbidden to light a flame on Sabbath, this dish is prepared Friday well before sundown set on a low flame (or put in a slow-cooker) and simmered overnight. Like *gefilte* fish, you either love it or hate it.

Blintzes
A crêpe that's usually filled with sweetened farmer cheese and/or fruit such as cherry or apple. Served with a little *smetnah* (sour cream).

Pierogen
Potato and onion dumplings. Usually fried in onions—what else?!

·····From the deli
Fun di vurshteray

Kosher and kosher-style Jewish delis usually have a full range of *wursts*, cured meats (pastrami, corned beef, tongue, etc.), roast chicken and turkey, as well as traditional Jewish treats such as…

Knish
Knishes are savory pastries, round or square, filled with anything from potato, cabbage, cheese, *kasha*, or even meat.

Kishke
Aka "stuffed derma," *kishke* means "guts." It's basically *matzoh* meal, fat, and spices, stuffed into a natural sausage casing (i.e., intestines), then sliced, fried, and served with gravy. True Jewish soul food!

Holishkes
Cabbage leaves filled with meat and/or rice, rolled tight and cooked in a simple tomato sauce, often with raisins.

Gedempteh fleish
Pot roast. Often served with potatoes and/or roasted root veggies.

Flanken
Beef short ribs

Shnitzel
A breaded chicken or veal cutlet. The Israeli fried chicken.

·····Dessert
Farbaysn

Dessert is a very important component of the Jewish meal. A rule of thumb for any family or holiday gathering is: one type of dessert for each person. At any Jewish wedding or bar mitzvah, the most talked about part of the affair is the "Viennese Table" piled high with a multitude of pastries and sweets.

Cake
Kukhen

Coffee cake
Kaveh kukhen

Sponge cake
Tawrt

Honey cake
Honig lehkekh

Cheese cake
Kez kukhen

Carrot cake
Mehren kukhen

Cookies
Kukhehlekh

Mandelbrot
Almond biscotti

THE KOSHER DELI)))
DER KASHER VURSTERAY

Give a Jew a choice between sex and a great pastrami sandwich, and nine times outta ten, cured meat is gonna win. If you want some nice pastrami, you'd better hurry up and find a kosher deli fast, because they are going the way of the buffalo.

Kosher delis are *fleishig*, meaning they serve meat products (and thus, no dairy). You could get yourself some corned beef, hot dogs, or salami as well as *parve* treats such as *latkes*, *kishke*, or *knishes*. Maybe wash it all down with a Dr. Brown's Celery Soda.

"Send a salami to your boy in the army" was the '40s-era slogan of Katz's delicatessen, on Manhattan's lower east side. Founded in 1888, the deli and the sign are still there, at the corner of Houston and Ludlow Streets. It's one of the few remaining kosher or kosher-style delis in New York. Katz's was where Meg Ryan had her fake orgasm in *When Harry Met Sally*. That table has a plaque to commemorate it, so you can sit there and "have what she had."

Another big player in New York's Pastrami Game is The Second Avenue Deli. Originally located on 2nd Avenue and 10th Street, it thrived in the old heart of the Yiddish theater district. A Yiddish Walk of Fame on the sidewalk out front commemorates the big stars of that era: Molly Picon, Menasha Skulnik, and the great actor Boris Thomashevsky (grandfather of celebrated conductor Michael Tilson-Thomas). Tragedy struck in March 2006 when the beloved owner, Abe Lebewohl, was robbed and murdered while bringing the day's receipts to the bank. As of this writing, the murder has not been solved. The deli, now run by other family members, has since moved from its old location to a new home at "Tirty Tird n' Tird" (33rd Street and 3rd Avenue).

And of course, there's Ben's kosher deli, with locations in midtown, Long Island, and the outer boroughs. And by outer boroughs, I mean Boca Raton.

Macaroons

Flourless coconut cookies, plain or flavored with almond, chocolate, vanilla, and other additions. *Kosher l'Pesach* (Kosher for Passover).

Hamentashen

A triangular cookie filled with jam, marzipan, prune compote, sweetened poppy seeds, or contemporary twists such as peanut butter and jelly or chocolate.

Pastries
Gehbeks

Teiglakh

Marble-size dough-balls, mounded high and drizzled in honey-syrup.

Babka

A yeasty coffee cake flavored with chocolate or cinnamon. *Seinfeld* based an entire episode on the relative merits of cinnamon vs. chocolate *babka*.

Rugelach

Chocolate, cinammon and sugar, or jam-filled pastries made from a cream cheese–based dough.

Stroodl

Strudel. Baked fruit, jam, nuts and spices, and/or sweetened cream cheese rolled into a fine layer of dough and baked to perfection.

Rice pudding
Riz kugel

Ice cream
Iz-krem

Fruit
Frukht

Sherbert
Frukht-iz

·····Oh! Am I thirsty!
Oy! Bin Ikh darstik!

An old man is sitting at the back of a crowded bus, jam-packed with passengers. "*Oy*, am I thirsty…! *Oyyyyyy*, ammmm Illll thirsty…" he *kvetches* loudly, non-stop. Ten, twenty, thirty minutes go by, and he's still complaining. Everyone on the bus can hear him and he's driving the other passengers *mishuggeh*! Finally, somebody begs the bus driver to stop the bus so they can get this man a drink. They pull into a rest stop and somebody runs in and brings him a big bottle of water. He drinks the entire bottle without coming up for air. The bus pulls out and everybody breathes a sigh of relief. Suddenly, from the backseat, "*Oy*, vaz I thirsty."

A glass of…
A glaz…
Note: There is no Yiddish "of" in such a phrase.

milk.
milkh.

water.
vasser.

seltzer.
greps vasser.
Literally, "burp water."

soda.
sodeh.

fruit drink.
frukht gehtrank. [frukht geh-TRAHNK]

tea.
tay.
Tea is traditionally served in a glass, as in Russia, Turkey, central Asia, and throughout the Arab world. Old-timers sip this strong black tea through a sugar cube clenched between their front teeth.

Coffee...
Kaveh...

> **with milk.**
> *mit milkh.*

> **with cream.**
> *mit krem.*

> **with sugar.**
> *mit tsuker.*

THE EGG CREAM)))
ECK KREM

Despite its name, it contains neither eggs nor cream. (Go figure!) So, just what is an egg cream? It's the perfect summer thirst-quencher: it was the Frappuccino of its day, made of milk, seltzer, and a squirt of Fox's UBet Chocolate Syrup. Any other kind of syrup, with one exception (see below), and it's not authentic! It must be consumed immediately upon serving, before the bubbles and foam dissipate.

Back in the days of soda fountains, serving up the perfect egg cream was essential to the success of any candy shop or luncheonette. Fortunes were made and broken by the ability to combine the best ingredients in the most satisfying proportions.

Louis Auster was, for a long time, the "King of the New York Egg Cream." Cabbies *shlepped* out-of-towners to his place on Second Avenue and 7th Street for a taste of real New York. In the basement of his diner, he concocted his own special chocolate syrup using a formula more closely guarded than Coca-Cola's. Legend has it that a national ice cream chain offered Auster an insultingly insignificant amount of money for the rights to the Egg Cream. Auster told them to buzz off, racial epithets ensued, and Auster vowed to take his secret recipe along with the origins of the name, to his grave. He didn't exactly do that. The secrets were passed on to his son, Mendy, who took them to his grave. Sadly, the last batch of their secret syrup was made in 1974.

·····Food-related proverbs and sayings
Esn veltsvertl

Love is sweet, but it's good with bread.
Di liebe iz zeiss nor zi iz gut mit broit.

Troubles with soup are easier than troubles without soup.
Tsuris mit yoykh iz gringer vi tsuris on yoykh.

You can't make cheesecakes out of snow.
Mit shnay ken men nit makhn gomolkhes.

Don't count your chickens before they hatch.
Patsh zikh nit in boykheleh ven fisheleh iz nokh in teikheleh.
Literally, "Don't rub your belly when the fish is still in the pond."
Note the almost-rhyme in Yiddish.

Everything revolves around bread and death.
Alts drait zikh arum broit un toyt.

·····In the restaurant
In der restauran

When it comes to food, quantity often compensates for lack of quality. The classic Jewish restaurant review: "The food was terrible! And in such small portions!"

Where is there a good kosher restaurant?
Voo iz dau a guteh kasherer [KASH-air-er] restauran?

The server
Der kelner/Di kelnehren

Bring me the menu!
Brengt mir dem mehnew!

What's the house specialty?
Vos is di spetsyalitet [spehts-yah-lee-TET] fun restauran?

iN A CHiNESE RESTAURANT)))
IN A KHINEZISH RESTAURAN

The old saw goes, "If you want to know if you're in a Jewish neighborhood, count the Chinese restaurants." Growing up on Long Island, in the '60s, our Sunday night dinner was always at Jade Garden. There was often a long wait to get a table because every other Jewish family in the neighborhood was also salivating for Mr. Eng's Cantonese.

Considering that shrimp and pork, two Chinese restaurant staples, are decidedly un-kosher, perhaps it's a bit odd that Jews love Chinese food. Or maybe it's precisely the lure of the exotic and forbidden that's so tempting and the siren call of greasy spare ribs and uber-*treyf* shrimp with lobster sauce.

Even some observant Jews were known to "cheat" on Sunday, as long as the *treyf* wasn't brought back into the home to "sully" their kosher dishware.

Perhaps it's as Philip Roth suggested in *Portnoy's Complaint*: In a Chinese restaurant, Jews didn't feel like "others." To their waiters, who were more "other" than they were, they were just generic white folk.

Another (totally true-to-life) cliché: On Christmas Day, Jews go to the movies, then out for Chinese. Traditionally, at least until the influx of other kinds of Asian cuisine, Chinese restaurants were the only ones open on the holiday and movie theaters usually had shorter lines.

A joke: A Jewish family is eating in a Chinese restaurant. Their young waiter, recently off the boat from China, speaks to them in perfect Yiddish. Curious, the father calls over the owner to inquire how this young man is able to speak Yiddish so well.

"Shhhh!" says the owner. "He thinks we're teaching him English!"

I didn't order this!
Ikh hob dos nit bahshtelt!

Check, please!
Dem kheshben, zayt azoy gut.

Keep the change.
Halt dem resht fahr zikh.

·····About the author

Adrienne Gusoff is a freelance writer, humorist, teacher, and lecturer. She is the creator and owner of BubbyGram (bubbygram.com), a party entertainment service. Started in 1983 as a singing-telegram company, Adrienne would dress up as a Jewish Grandma and *shlep* all over the New York tri-state area in drag, delivering birthday bagels and get-well chicken soup, performing her original songs, jokes, and shtick. As her character, she has been featured on international TV, radio, in magazines and newspapers.

She is the creator and writer of Bubby Greeting Cards (Recycled Paper Greetings), as well as other humorous card lines for many different card publishers. She teaches Greeting Card Design and Marketing at Parsons/The New School in New York City. She is the author of Zen Jewish Jokes and Lucky in Love, among other books. She is also a hypnotist and life coach, lecturing and writing on the subject of love and relationships (artofepiphany.com). She holds a B.S. in Communications/Journalism from Boston University.

Adrienne lives in New York with her husband, Michael Berkowitz, a real *mensch* and a brilliant artist and photographer *mit goldeneh hends*.